THE
PERMISSIVE
SOCIETY

FACT OR FANTASY?

THE PERMISSIVE SOCIETY

FACT OR FANTASY?

John Selwyn Gummer

CASSELL · LONDON

CASSELL & COMPANY LTD
35 Red Lion Square, London, WC1
Sydney, Auckland
Toronto, Johannesburg

First published 1971

I.S.B.N. 0 304 93821 1

Printed in Great Britain by
The Camelot Press Ltd, London and Southampton
F.671

Contents

Acknowledgements

To write a book about The Permissive Society and avoid the twin dangers of mere reaction on the one hand, and easy acceptance of fashionable views on the other, is an extremely difficult task. If I have been in any way successful, it has been largely through the advice of the many people who have helped me in this work. I should particularly mention Leon Brittan, Michael Marshall, and my brother, Mark, who read the manuscript; Jo Carver who organized it; and Win Cox who typed it.

This book is dedicated to my father.

1 How Permissive?

Permissiveness is, more often than not, a term of abuse used by one generation for all those things it dislikes in another. As a phrase intended as an insult but seized upon by some as a compliment, the permissive society almost defies definition. It is certainly a handy cover for all those things which the conventional dislike. It can comprehend anything from nude bathing to ritual murder, from girly magazines to TV violence. As such it can simply be dismissed as the modern term for those changes in society which happen every generation and of which a band of sterner—and older—moralists always disapprove.

Indeed there are many who have sought to prove that today's society is very much like any other and that the usual strife between the fashionable and the old-fashioned has merely been heightened by the increased economic importance of youth which has tilted the balance more decisively against the traditionalist. In support of this view, the denunciations of moralists from every age have been quoted to show that Pope Paul, Mrs Whitehouse, and Senator Keating have a long series of historical counterparts. Some of these early Jeremiahs have been dusted down after centuries of obscurity and toted out to prove that nothing ever changes. By quoting Peter the Hermit's denunciation of students to Young Conservatives from all over Britain, Geoffrey Johnson Smith gave the old moralist a reputation he hasn't enjoyed since the Middle Ages—all to bring home the undoubted fact that every generation fears that the old order passes and that the new is a very inferior substitute.

Those who play down the change in the manners of our society suggest that the difference is merely that now we are open about things which once we used to hide. The advocates of this view believe that opposition to the permissive society comes from those who find hypocrisy comforting and who would far rather we brushed under the carpet anything unconventional. The former British Home Secretary, Roy Jenkins, believes that Western society is more open and tolerant rather than more permissive. We do what we have always done but we do it less secretively and guiltily and we are therefore more able to tolerate those who do not act in accordance with convention. As the Victorian public stance was so very different from our own, it is vitally important for the proponents of the 'no change' view that their private actions must be shown to be as like our own as possible. *Newsweek*'s review of Stephen Morris's *The Other Victorians*, which has been widely used in advertising the book, gleefully said: 'By sex obsessed . . . heaves back the cold, rock-like exterior of Victorian England and beneath is enough teeming sexuality to satiate a dozen Kinseys'. A good case for this can be made out. The prostitution statistics were enormous. In London, with a population in 1870 of just over three million, it was said there were anything up to 80,000 prostitutes. Every capital city had its villas built by the well-to-do for their lady friends. Victorian erotica—books like *The Pearl*, *My Secret Life*, and *Walter*—all show clearly that there were 'the other Victorians'. The famous cases of Oscar Wilde, Charles Dilke and Parnell certainly point to a side of nineteenth-century life which the mores presented in the novels of the period would hardly make one suspect. We can easily take the Victorians at their own estimation of themselves and forget that there were less genteel sides of nineteenth-century life. So too, harking back to the 'good old days' can be a way of disguising one's envy. A great deal of the criticism of today's manners comes from those whose real trouble is their frustration and regret for lost youth. They see young people having it a good deal better than they did and find the situation very hard to accept. They tend to ignore the fact that although for some generations before our own, people were much less open about sex and much more inhibited about acknowledging enjoyment, they did not entirely miss out on either. While Bowdler made Shakespeare fit for family reading, Boucicault happily hinted at all kinds of merry romps; despite public censure George Eliot determinedly pursued her extra-marital love-match; and Lord Alfred Douglas was hardly inhibited by the Labouchère amendment—either at home or abroad.

Nevertheless, this is only part of the story. There *has* been a real change in society since the Second World War. This is more fundamental than either the novelties to which in every generation the young flock and the old object, or the mere change to a society prepared to admit publicly the things which privately have always been true. The nineteenth century was a period in which the prevailing attitude was one of economic permissiveness and moral repression. The twentieth century has increasingly reversed that position, and restricted and cosseted us economically while leaving us more and more free to do as we like in bed.

For a century after the Industrial Revolution, only the most rudimentary regulations inhibited a manufacturer from carrying on his business in the manner he thought fit. He could build his factory wherever he could buy the land, employ his labour in almost any conditions, get rid of his effluent in whatever way he wished, and exaggerate the claims made for his product to almost any extent. There was no Food and Drugs Commission; only the most basic Factory Acts; no Advertising Standards Committee; and no conservation lobby. As a result men drugged themselves throughout the U.S.A. with laudanum and other opium derivatives and made London famous for its smoke-filled bronchial fogs. Women died of phossy-jaw in match factories and from haemorrhages caused by patent medicines which claimed, oh so discreetly, to produce miscarriages. It is no wonder that the poet, Gerard Manley Hopkins saw a world where: 'All is seared with trade; bleared, smeared with toil; And wears man's smudge and shares man's smell.'

Of course, just as man could do almost what he liked while he was on his way up, so too he was permitted to fall as far as he wished when he failed. When his success had run out, Hudson, the railway king, had as much freedom to starve as any of the labourers who had built his mighty bridges and embankments.

The principle of self-help implied the possibility of self-destruction and the exercise of free will in the economic sphere was a basic dogma of the new industrial state. The material well-being of society would be best served by the free play of economic forces. Yet its spiritual welfare could not be left to free choice. Morality was a social necessity: society could be neither prosperous nor settled unless its citizens were good.

The Industrial Revolution had meant that men had to work long hours in disciplined conditions very different from those obtaining in an agricultural environment. A disciplined work force was the essential basis for nineteenth-century growth. The manufacturer as entrepreneur responded to the market needs but it was his solid achievement as the organizer of labour and machines which satisfied them. It was therefore no wonder that hard work became the first among Victorian virtues. The devil would certainly find work for idle hands to do, for idleness and immorality were closely linked. Private morality was therefore essential to public good. Drunkenness was seen, not as a *symptom* of the hopelessness of the depressed working classes, but as the *cause* of their state. The Band of Hope and the other temperance societies believed that the regulation of Man's private morals was essential not only for his own good but for that of society. It was not surprising, therefore, that so many of the temperance songs had a patriotic flavour, linking the personal victory over drink to the national glory.

> We're a Temperance army, dear friends come and aid us
> We're working to make England sober and free
> For the love of our country we're banded together
> In rank we march forward while singing with glee
> Dear fathers and mothers, dear sisters and brothers
> And uncles and cousins from drink dangers flee.

There was of course a certain truth in all this. In any age without any form of Welfare State, it was the sober who were thrifty and it was the thrifty who were best able to tide themselves over hard times.

Yet to the Victorian this would have seemed too utilitarian a view. It was not just that the thriftless lost such money as they did have—it was that private immorality corrupted society and that personal goodness was socially desirable. More than that they saw it as one of society's duties that it should encourage morality as being essential for the State. There was no question of the State opting out of the judgement of private moral actions. As these affected society, so they should come within the ambit of the law.

This attitude was taken to enormous lengths. John Keble, one of the greatest of Victorian Churchmen and a leader of the Catholic revival in the Church of England, enjoyed a considerable reputation as a poet. He was quite clear that 'only a good man could write good poetry'. Morality really was basic even to a poet's efficient functioning! It was therefore the State's job to see that private morality was encouraged.

Today we are much more preoccupied with a man's economic effect on others and we increasingly deny, at least in theory, that private sin makes for public danger. Whereas the Victorians believed that the State had to be restrictive in the field of private moral actions or society would suffer, we believe that a man's private life is his own and the State need take no account of it.

Yet we are, of course, much less permissive than the Victorians in almost every other field. We constrain business enterprise, employment conditions, advertising standards, and building proposals. We protect the individual from every possible material harm which may come to him. Not only is there the full panoply of the Welfare State in most Western European nations which protect a man lest he should be sick, unemployed or redundant; we also see that he is not tricked by doorstep salesmen, misled by food packagers, or poisoned by additives and impurities. We protect him from the results of his ignorance, lest he should not be able to read the small print on an agreement; from the results of his folly, in case he should have spent all his money and have none for his old age; and from the results of his continuing bad habits, by providing subsidized medical treatment for him when his smoking has caused lung cancer, bronchitis or heart disease. On every side we extend and improve our regulations to protect the citizen from material harm and restrict his freedom of material decision. We are as restrictive materially as the Victorians were morally.

We are, of course, also becoming more restrictive in some non-material ways. The emphasis on preservation and conservation has led most countries to produce planning laws embodying criteria which go well beyond the hard material facts of industrial zoning, density, and building stress-factors. New construction must harmonize with its surroundings, areas of outstanding beauty—natural or man-made—must be protected, structures out of keeping with local standards cannot be erected. The 'anti-ugly' campaigns in Britain in the early sixties have blossomed into full scale preservationist battles in Europe and America. The middle-class matrons whose concern was to 'keep Virginia green' have now been joined by tens of thousands of young campaigners talking ecology and environment. Their language owes more to science than to sentimentalists like Ella Wheeler Wilcox and their methods involve precisely that restriction of individual liberty which has come to be accepted as essential in governing the material side of our lives. They demand that no man has a right to make the world ugly for his fellows. Increasingly our society is accepting that the quality of the environment in which men live can greatly influence the way in which they behave and the quality of their lives and it is therefore the duty of the State to encourage a good environment.

Now no part of what I have said should be construed as an attack upon welfare, consumer protection, or conservation. It is merely to point out that when we talk of the permissive society we cannot simply assume that society has become less restrictive throughout. Indeed the opposite is in fact true. The twentieth century permits a great deal less than did the nineteenth and only in the sphere of private morality is it more permissive.

We have therefore become less restrictive if not less censorious. During the Profumo affair in Great Britain, a great deal of energy was expended by public commentators in explaining that it was his lie to the House of Commons and the possible danger to national security because of his liaison with Christine Keeler that was being criticized—not in any way his adultery. The Victorians would have made no bones about it. They would have said quite clearly that public men should set an example in private morality. They would have seen such behaviour as harmful *per se*. This was certainly the reaction of the majority of the population of Britain even in 1963. He had no business to behave like that—a reaction which can hardly have differed from that of the Victorian man in the street. Yet articulate opinion has certainly changed. Publicly we believe that a man's private actions are his own affair because they do not harm society in any measurable way. As this is so we see no reason to restrict private behaviour by law, particularly as many of our attempts to do so have been relatively unsuccessful. We have adopted the useful distinction between sin and crime and the legal framework of most Western nations now permits much which it once banned.

Of course, we have found it hard to know where to draw the line. When does private action become public? How do we protect the young and feeble-minded—or do we protect them at all? How important is family life to the security of the State and how is it threatened by private immorality? What about private immorality which puts a cost upon the State? Beyond all these questions are two fundamental ones. First, what duties can the State properly ask of its citizens; and second, do we need a total reappraisal of morality. Is that which we have always thought to be wrong, actually wrong?

In the nineteenth century, men had few such worries. They accepted that the State had a duty to uphold morality and that private morality ought to be subject to the law as it affected society. They then experienced little difficulty in deciding of what private morality consisted. There was a consensus— at least among the articulate. People knew what the standards were and knew when they and, more particularly, others were falling short of them.

Today there is no such consensus. The traditional moral standards of Western Christian civilization are not merely found difficult or merely ignored—they are actively challenged. This is the second basic reason why the permissive society which we are creating differs fundamentally from those societies which have preceded it. If on the level of law we have reversed an order which was morally repressive and materially permissive, so on a philosophic level we have challenged tenets of morality which have been held in our society for centuries.

They were tenets which were, of course, often broken but their validity was not challenged by any but a tiny minority. Even in the turbulent times of the Commonwealth, only the Ranters turned morality on its head. Throughout the Middle Ages nobody seriously questioned the moral rules of the Church. Many broke them and most tried to excuse their transgression but they were perfectly aware that they had sinned. Even in the rationalist eighteenth century, Boswell did not claim that his amatory exploits were moral. He merely thought them excusable and fun. It is twentieth-century Man who has begun to suggest that there is a new morality which in many respects runs counter to the old. In this claim he has been joined by some of his 'priests' who, in former years at least, continued to

preach the old morality even if they failed to practise it. Now
some are preaching the new, although for the most part practising the old!

Here then is our starting point in examining the permissive
society. It is a unique situation in that, at a time of unprece-
dented legal restriction upon Man's material behaviour,
Western societies are increasingly permitting citizens to make
their own private moral decisions. At the same time, these
private moral decisions are being made in a society where
traditional moral constraints are losing their hold as more and
more articulate people condemn the Judaeo-Christian code
and propose replacements.

In these circumstances it is not surprising that the scene is
characterized by confusion rather than order. There are certain
issues where most Western nations are beginning to produce a
common legal answer. Birth control methods are increasingly
made freely available and countries are less likely to imprison
homosexuals. In general, divorce laws are becoming less restrictive, attempted suicide is now rarely punishable, and censorship
of obscenity has lost its former rigidity. Nevertheless, even in
these areas where the general trend is clear, the pattern is certainly not uniform. Britain will probably tighten up her abortion
laws, Spain continues to maintain strict moral censorship,
Ireland prohibits divorce on any ground, the French continue
to restrict the dissemination of birth control information and
in America some states remain untouched by the permissive
trend in legislation.

Still more contentious are those issues where the battle lines
are less predictable and where even the 'progressives' themselves
have not made up their minds whether certain private actions
harm the public interest. Foremost among these is the State's
attitude to drugs and drug-taking, but there is also the question
of the censorship of violence and restrictions upon men's racial
views and attitudes. What too should we do about incest and
euthanasia? In all these there is not even the beginning of a
common Western answer. Each group of issues will have to be
discussed separately but there are, even amidst the apparent
confusion, two general tendencies worth noting.

There is, first, a close interrelation between the issues. The
advocates of one kind of relaxation tend to support the others.

People who select one issue upon which they are actively 'liberal' while holding traditionalist views on others are in the minority. One is expected to join the liberals wholeheartedly and any reservations are usually put down to some personal consideration which clouds one's reasoning. This is really a result of the second general factor which is that the demand for most of the permissive changes in legislation has been a limited one, confined to an articulate group and rarely gaining the support of the 'silent majority'. It is difficult to discern any widespread desire in any Western country for the abolition of the laws governing pornography yet in most countries there is an active and well-organized pressure group to do just this. Most changes in moral legislation have been put through without forming any significant part of the ruling party's election manifesto. Indeed where such legislation was put to the people, as in Italy in 1970 on the divorce question, they voted even more strongly for parties opposing the liberal position. Usually, however, there is no opportunity for the public to choose. In Denmark the Conservative coalition government which removed all censorship on pornographic literature, not only did so without any mandate from its electorate, but it announced its decision without any vote in Parliament.

It would of course be foolish to suggest that Parliament should never lead but should always follow popular demand. It is, however, important to realize that it is the attitude of the élite which has changed towards moral legislation, not that of the majority. This élite—which the journalist, the late Robert Pitman used to call 'The Lilac Establishment'—is quite as arbitrary and dictatorial as its traditional forerunners. It believes, like any good pressure group, that it knows best and that the public will soon get over their opposition. Steve Abrams, the American campaigner for the legalization of cannabis, claimed that there were three hundred people in Britain that you had to convince in order to change the law. President Nixon's dismissal of the Commission's report on pornography is clearly done in the belief that only the articulate minority support it, so too was the angry denunciation by the former British Home Secretary, James Callaghan, of the Wootton Report on drugs. Indeed, there is an inevitable arrogance among liberal pressure groups which ill accords with the

B

demands for democratic control which the same people are wont to make in other circumstances and in discussing other countries like Greece and South Africa. This attitude of knowing best was of course equally true of the traditionalist élite of former years but at least they were not inconsistent. They never claimed that their case had to rest on popular support. They were right either because they acted according to divine injunction or because they thought that society ought to be regulated by right-thinking people and an example ought to be set by the leaders of the nation. Their position may not have been any more justifiable than that of the Lilac Establishment but it was at least honest.

Today the professional liberals are rightly alarmed at the way in which the Western democracies seem unable to involve the population effectively in their decision-making. They naturally look at the totalitarian developments in Greece and elsewhere and do all they can to restore democracy. There is, however, little pressure for participation when it comes to decisions in the moral sphere. John Calder, eloquent opponent of dictators though he may be, is nonetheless not noticeably concerned that his views on obscenity are not shared by the majority of his countrymen. Tony Palmer, writing in the London *Spectator*, attacked the young people of London who had overwhelmingly opposed his liberal views on a radio programme. He agreed that they represented majority opinion but said 'majority opinion is usually wrong'. This is also the attitude of American underground newspapers as it is that of the European Marcusian Left.

Now there is no fundamental reason why legislative changes should have the support of the majority at the time they are made. A government must do what it thinks right on behalf of the nation and then present itself at regular intervals for the nation to pass general judgment. All that we should note is that the liberal élite is acting in precisely the way that it finds so objectionable in other élites with whose views it disagrees and it behaves with the same assurance of the rightness of its cause that it finds so nauseating in the Victorians or in an older generation.

It also demands a conformity of view which is surprising. It seems that particularly in America, but also in Europe, the liberal ticket on moral legislation is a predictable one even though the issues themselves are so diverse and might perhaps require differing answers. It seems to come as a surprise that an opponent of capital punishment might carry his views on the sanctity of human life as far as supporting anti-abortion laws. The progressive is also expected to laugh at the laws which censor obscene literature on the grounds that it is so difficult to decide what is obscene. Yet he must support strongly, laws designed to censor racialist literature. It is evidently much easier to decide when something is racially suspect; although Britain's experience with laws which stopped the Welsh Church advertising for Welsh clergy to serve in Welsh-speaking parishes or which made children's books with black golliwogs very dubious, might give one leave to doubt it. There is, nonetheless, among the progressives a polarizing tendency which produces a conformity of view on a wide range of causes and tends to suggest that departure from this line is automatically reactionary.

So too, on the other side, the continuing effect of the liberal propagandists leads many to feel that the only defence against the implementation of every point of the progressive programme is to oppose it root and branch. That which is clearly absurd is supported merely because it is the *status quo* with no attempt to distinguish between traditional nonsense and traditional wisdom. It is therefore all the more important that the issues should be examined separately. It may well be that enlightenment has not come exclusively to one side or the other and that there is logic in some of the causes espoused by Miss Vanessa Redgrave but not in all, and that although Spiro Agnew is manifestly silly on some issues he is not automatically so on all.

What, however, must be accepted is that we *have* a right and purpose to discuss the issues. The liberal propagandists do tend to imply that it is merely a matter of time before they win and that opposition to any of their causes is merely a rearguard action with no hope of success. It is a sort of extension of the Whig interpretation of history, suggesting that all civilization is moving towards a permissive attitude and that it is merely those who yearn for the days gone by who oppose this inexorable march. It is the pious belief of all élitist establishments. The Victorians certainly thought that all before was barbarism, gradually giving way to the light. They often excused the works of earlier authors on the grounds that the manners of the time were imperfect. Thus when the Restoration dramatists were republished in a complete form reviewers accepted their bawdiness in much the same way that they might excuse the actions of a savage people who had not yet reached their perfection of civilization. This indulgence came from the assurance that all history had led to the state of perfection of manners which characterized the Victorian age.

The same assurance can be seen today among the progressive élite. The impression given is that their views are bound to triumph because the tide of history is with them. This natural stance of the righteous intellectual is only dangerous because those responsible for mass communication tend to believe it. They, therefore, wishing to show themselves on the side of the light, present the proponents of permissiveness as intellectual lions and those who disagree, either as buffoons, biased by their intellectual inferiority, or as reactionaries whose views do not count because they bring religion into them, or are swayed by personal experiences. So Leo Abse's refusal to support whole-sale abortion in Britain, while contininug to back the progres-sive causes in which he has played so prominent a part, is laughed off as an aberration, while Fr Hill is characterized as a religious fanatic. Sometimes, of course, they are so sure that the progressives will triumph that they merely present that side of the case. When a number of British Members of Parliament signed a motion regretting the staging of *Oh! Calcutta!* in London the B.B.C. News merely recorded an interview with *avant garde* publisher, John Calder, attacking the motion. It was not considered necessary that any of the signatories should be interviewed, despite the fact that they had, but a month before, been elected to represent their constituents whereas Mr Calder primarily represented a small group of interested parties, some of whom would gain directly from the relaxation of censorship laws.

Examples abound of this assurance that the progressives are right and logical and that their opponents are wrong and emotional. It is assumed throughout this book that neither this nor the reverse is true.

A great deal of reactionary foolishness is talked by those whose opposition to the permissive society is rooted in their dislike of change. Like Goldsmith's Hardcastle they would say, 'I love everything that's old; old friends, old times, old manners, old books, old wines' and newness is to them anathema. Yet in the same way 'the new' must not become synonymous with 'the good'. That something is new tells us no more about its value than if we were told it was old. The fact that the permissive society is a departure from previous practice should not prejudice us one way or the other. Instead we should be concerned to see what sort of society this will produce and how best it can be made into a valuable environment in which the citizen can fully reach his potential.

We must start with the genesis of the permissive attitude— how has it arisen and how far is it a common phenomenon in the Western nations. Should there in fact be legal restraint upon private morals and are there any grounds upon which Western society can properly look to a moral code in ordering its public affairs? Can it require its citizens to conform to any standard of private behaviour and what should that standard be?

2 The Growth of Permissiveness

The progressive interpretation of history provides for liberals a handy explanation for the emergence of the permissive society. It is seen as the flowering of freedom after the dark years of superstitious restriction. It is the final justification of that apostolic succession of rationalists who braved the Victorian era. According to this theory the lifting of restrictions and the change of attitudes is the result of the long battle against traditionalism. It is not therefore surprising that the British magistrate, Lady Wootton, chose a quotation from John Stuart Mill to introduce her Report on drugs. She had not of course gone as far in her recommendations as the progressives might have hoped but she certainly saw the Report as part of an historical pattern in which the traditional moral values were replaced by the rational considerations pioneered in earlier years against tremendous opposition. It is as if our present age had finally grasped the truth of the Victorian rationalists.

In fact the major reasons for the change in attitudes can be found in the social and economic changes since the Second World War. We now have a society in which it is possible and easy to be permissive whereas this was once not so. Curiously enough, far from being a vindication of the rationalists' approach, the way in which society has changed would have horrified them. The moral seriousness which characterized their attitudes and their writings and which Lady Wootton and some of her generation share, would have been outraged by the fact that society has become more free largely because the young have become the prime target of the advertising man and the marketeer.

Throughout the Western world the period since the war has seen the rise of a free-spending younger generation with, relatively, much more in its pocket than ever before. Affluence has brought with it a profound change in the family structure and social habits of young people who have been made

economically important for the first time. The great mass of consumer advertising is aimed at exactly this section of the market
which, between fifteen and thirty, will have fewer ties and more
flexibility in expenditure than any other.

Formerly these young people would have earned little and
worked long hours. Today they earn well, they have benefited
from the general reduction in the working week, and they have
fewer essential calls upon their pay packets than their seniors.
To this section of the community the advertisers beam every
possible inducement to spend and it is their needs and even
more their caprices which the marketing experts eagerly study
as they plan new products.

It has of course always been true that new fashions and new
ideas have been taken up by young people. In previous generations the young sprigs of the ruling classes certainly provided a
living for those whose business it was to provide fashionable
novelties. Whether it was the Regency buck, the aesthetic
Tractarian curate, or the Great Gatsby himself, the new and
the unusual found a ready acceptance. These, however,
represented a much smaller market and their tastes spread, if
spread they did, much more slowly down through the population. There is a mass market for novelty. As David Ogilvy
has shown us, the most effective word in the advertisers'
vocabulary is *new*. There is also a whole section of the population
with money to spend and whose age makes it naturally more
disposed than most to react to the attraction of newness.

It is not surprising, therefore, that this growing concentra-
tion upon the youthful market has helped to create a feeling of
identity within it and has confirmed a natural belief in its
own importance. If the advertisers of soft drinks are determined
to spend a good deal of money in identifying their product with
young people of the Pepsi-generation, it is not surprising that
those same young people should become, at least subconsciously,
aware of the fact that they are important.

In concentrating on the youthful market, the advertisers
have also been concerned to identify their products with the
values of that generation and have therefore served to reinforce
young people's belief that not only are they important but that
their *attitudes* matter—perhaps even that their attitudes matter
more than those of any other section of the community. It must

be expected that American banks will continue to print cheques promoting 'protest' views and milk will go on improving hippie beauty so long as these are the interests of this the prime target for advertisers.

Thus for the first time the young people in our society have become corporately more important economically than any other group in the population. This tendency is bound to increase as industry becomes ever more marketing-oriented. The attitudes and values of the young will be continually held up as admirable by advertisers who need to gain the approbation of this section of the community if they are to tap the rich market which they represent.

Yet even more fundamental is the change in the leadership of fashion which has occurred so recently. It was once true that fashion in almost everything was dictated from the top of the social hierarchy and gradually made its way down, being modified for reasons of utility or expense. Today the fashionable market is the mass market and as it is reached instantly, it dictates the fashions. It is the Twiggys and the pop groups, the personalities and the photographers, who set the seal on a successful vogue, a vogue which is all the more instant because, thanks to mass production and the ready availability of cash, the market is immediately able to follow. Even the exclusive world of *haute couture* is really kept going from profits made by the great designers in the mass market. Once the rich made and paid for the changes in fashion—today the change comes from below and the rich are increasingly either the designer's hobby and creative outlet or merely part of his public relations machine.

Now there is nothing deplorable in itself about this change in fashion. It does, however, have certain far-reaching consequences. It means that fashion is directed almost exclusively by the young for the young. Its increasingly instant nature and the demands of the mass market place an even greater premium upon the transient and the soon-outmoded. The market may be superficially sophisticated but it is hardly discriminating. Above all it is the least educated who are the most important. Those who stay on at school and then continue at college have much less spending power than those who go out to work as early as it is legal to do so. Moreover, the kind of jobs which are available to the less well educated and the high-school drop-out are those which tend to pay best in the shortest time, while those for which further training is required tend to offer their rewards when some experience has been gained.

What we have then in the Western world, is a younger generation whose economic importance has become central to the marketing strategy of the major manufacturers of consumer products. This mass market creates fashion and tends to be dominated by the wants of the less well educated. They are, therefore, bound to be predisposed to regular and rapid change in taste and relatively unresistant to the aggrandisement of trivia into major matters of importance.

It is thus not surprising that the keynote of this world should be continuous movement and excitement. Its virtues are bound to be those of change and novelty, while continuity and order are necessarily thrust aside. The values are undemanding in anything save energy. They require neither discipline nor discrimination. The products are made to be discarded so there is little virtue in either workmanship or quality. The result is that young people exist in a culture where steadfastness and stability are not virtues to be despised—they merely don't exist. It would, therefore, be hard to expect this generation to demand from sexual relationships any virtues other than the variety and excitement which it seeks in its other activities, and which are continually reinforced by the millions of pounds spent by advertisers in wooing the young.

That is not to say that this is a bad generation. It is just a more difficult generation in which to grow up than we often suppose. We tend to believe that because the young are un-afflicted by the fears and cares of unemployment, low wages, and long working hours then they ought to be entirely better off than previous generations. This is to make precisely the kind of material measurement of which the anti-permissivists so often complain. We must, however, face up to the fact that we have created a society in which the young have gained an economic importance far beyond that of any previous period and for that reason the balance which society has in the past achieved has been upset. Previously there was the continuous tension between the virtue of stability which the old tended to uphold and the desire for change which the young more natur-ally favoured. Some societies have achieved that balance more effectively than others. What is certainly true is that the virtues of novelty will be increasingly insisted upon with a voice which seems likely to drown all other contenders.

Obviously a society in search of variety and excitement will not cling too tenaciously to moral taboos which surround sex, drugs and violence. This is particularly so when in the wake of the post-war social revolution has come the opportunity to break these moral taboos. The financial freedom of most young people has meant that their dependence upon the family grouping for existence has almost disappeared and with it has gone much parental authority. They know that their children can afford to leave home and that they then would lose such influence that remains to them and so they tend to give in rather than risk the final break which would mean the cessation of any influence at all. Not that some parents have been at pains to lose their influence at an earlier age. The belief that children should not be cramped by any restriction on their self-expression sometimes seems to have become the universal creed of motherhood. It is a convenient creed for the present age. Discipline of even the crudest type demands involvement and concern. The parents have to know their children and understand what they do. This takes time and is itself a restriction on the freedom of parents which ill accords with a society where often both work and both resent anything which stops their continued enjoyment of their own pleasures. Thus it is convenient to give the children their head—it saves the time involved in explaining why not; it stops one having to stay at home during boring adolescent parties; and above all it means one is never accused of 'spoiling their fun'.

Not that this kind of upbringing is proof against the natural desire of young people to leave home. Large numbers of them move into the sort of unbalanced community where the traditional values have very little chance of holding sway. Their financial independence makes it possible for them to choose to associate only with people of their own age. They share flats together, very often in the same areas of towns, and create a self-contained community which is unchallenged by others differing in age or experience. It is this community which is continually told how special and different it is by the advertisers and the mass media. In this way the natural tendency of any group, and of young people in particular, to feel itself unique and special, is increased.

This separation does provide the young, whether they are still in the parental home or not, with an opportunity for taking on different moral values from those professed by their parents. In the tightly-knit family grouping the opportunities for privacy are so limited that the sheer mechanics of being permissive are difficult to arrange. It is no wonder that Wilhelm Reich when writing his outspoken plea for sexual intercourse for all in *The Sexual Revolution*, spends a good deal of time showing that one of the prerequisites is privacy. Indeed he suggests that it is one of the first duties of parents to see that their children have proper accommodation in which to pursue their love affairs. Since the 1930s this problem has increasingly been overcome and the opportunities for permissive behaviour have multiplied!

This means opportunities both in the premeditated and the accidental sense. If a young man wants to sleep with his girl-friend then there is usually somewhere where they can do so undisturbed. The 'cad's pad' is not merely confined to the pages of spy fiction, although the furnishings are rarely as glamorous as those provided for Michael Caine. It is also true that it is much easier for one person to suggest that others join him in smoking cannabis if the party they are attending is unlikely to be interrupted by anyone except their own group. Thus, where-as it has always been possible to find a way to do as one wishes, our social conditions make it much easier even for those who would not otherwise have made the effort. It is therefore hardly surprising that when drug addicts, quoted in Louria's recent book, explained how they first took to drugs, time after time the circumstances described were of this protected kind.

What is generally true about young people is of course also true of the student population considered separately. By definition they tend to have rather less money to spend and are better educated than their counterparts already at work. However, they often become even more alienated from older generations than other young people. As increasing numbers of students come from homes where their parents were much less well educated, the intellectual gap between them and their parents can become enormous. The society in which they move at university or college is so different from that which obtains in their home town that their unsettled feelings and sense of not belonging are bound to increase. It is hardly surprising that older generations have little chance of passing on the views and values which they have learned through experience to trust. It is difficult for the student to see why his parents' mores apply to him, when every day he sees evidence of how much of his parents' life and thought is irrelevant or even unacceptable. He cannot despise their views on race, Vietnam, long hair, and student riots, and still be expected to take as gospel their attitudes to sex and religion. With the almost complete breakdown of the old teacher/student relationship the separation between the generations is almost complete and we seem practically to be back in the medieval situation with a body of students whose only allegiance is to each other and who feel no real connection with the outside world.

Thus youth, singled out as important by the commentators and the advertising men, is increasingly unfettered by the conventional sanctions which a balanced community imposes. It doesn't matter what Mrs Jones thinks because Mrs Jones doesn't know or care. What is more, because this youthful community has little contact with the older generation it has increasingly little reason to see why it should defer to the older generation's judgement. It is here that the oft discussed breakdown of authority becomes most apparent. The child increasingly has no financial dependence upon the family grouping. His society and its attitudes are so different from that of his parents. He may well be much better educated than they are and all the natural revolt of child against parent is reinforced by the lack of communication which this so often entails.

The isolation thus engendered makes the young look at the world exclusively from their own point of view, unadulterated by the attitudes and insights of other generations. They must, as a result, become increasingly concerned with the values which appeal to them as young people and have little reminder of those which are important to other sections of the community. The family and the State are particularly concerned with the values of stability and order, and the authority which either wields is designed to maintain both. Yet the community which the young creates has a vested interest in change and excitement. Formerly the two had to live side by side and the tension between them created necessary adjustments to society. Now we have a youthful community which is international. The young of one nation have much more in common with young people in other countries than with their own countrymen of a different generation. There really is a great divide and being a society within a society brings its own frustrations which result in a refusal to be involved and an understandable alienation.

We have then a disconnected generation with a strong self-identity and little sense of the importance or relevance of authority. The opportunity for accepting and practising a permissive morality is obviously great and the restraints minimal. Not only that but there is a perfectly respectable rationale at hand. The old taboos are the product of a totally different situation. They are necessary to uphold a society in which stability and security is important. They make for an environment which is conducive to continuity. Now these values can hardly have any relevance to a society which does not want to create this kind of environment. There is no particular reason to ban cannabis if you accept the excitement of an escape from reality as a major aim. The importance of a stable marriage partner is hardly crucial in a society where variety is the touchstone.

To people who argue thus, the opposition is clearly easy meat. Their objections are based upon arguments which have lost their bite as they have lost their religious basis. The middle class of Western society had got so used to professing the conventional moral code, it had begun to believe this was the expression of self-evident truths. It has therefore found it extremely difficult to argue with a new generation which finds the code unfitted to the sort of society which they can see being built around them. Parents and teachers 'knew' what was right and wrong and, until fairly recently, that knowledge was rarely challenged although its teaching was pretty widely evaded. The logic behind that knowledge was at best shaky and at worst non-existent. It has therefore become largely ignored.

This is the more so as there is an attractive alternative moral code available. This concentrates people's minds upon the immorality outside themselves. It points to the horrors of nuclear war, of world poverty, and of American action in

Vietnam. On a more mundane level it can focus attention upon students' rights and representation and landladies' racialism. As the older generation can be seen to be responsible for this immorality in world society, their moral code can easily look pretty sick. Getting worked up about smoking cannabis is fairly irrelevant when your friends are being sent off to the war in Vietnam or are being imprisoned for refusing the draft.

The great advantage of these sort of causes is that they have universal validity. They can appeal to young people throughout the world and spread from campus to campus without difficulty. They also put an older generation in a great quandary. There are many for whom the moral issues raised are real ones and they support the campaigns which result from them with the same simple and direct faith which characterizes the movements. For the majority, although the moral issues may be clear, the complications involved are also clear. How do we get out of Vietnam? What about Thailand, Burma, Laos, and Cambodia? Should we hold back our child by sending him to the local school to show that we are happy for him to mix with the largely coloured intake even though educational standards may seem lower? If we get rid of our bombs then what about the Russians? If we increase our aid, what about our balance of payments and how do we sell it to the ordinary taxpayer? All these are the questions of the involved and those who have responsibility. As such they can be simply answered by a generation which says that they are the kind of considerations which got the world into this mess and therefore they are invalid—'All you need is love'.

In a sense, therefore, it is perfectly reasonable that this generation should merely protest rather than become involved in providing an answer. The student radicals and their philosophical followers among the younger generation are making a comment on the morality of their seniors—'it stinks'. All the traditional moral values in the Western world have failed to answer world poverty, war, racialism, and oppression. In the face of that, pious words about purity, chastity, non-violence, and the dangers of drugs ring rather hollow.

This externalizing of the moral issues has of course the advantage that one can be on the side of the angels without overmuch trouble. Self-discipline need not play much part. For the majority it means holding a series of prescribed views with support for the occasional protest. For the leaders it may mean fighting the police, a prison sentence, or a fine. For everybody it provides a rationale for the new morality. These are the issues that count; it is on one's attitude to these that society should judge. Just as private morality is seen as having no effect on the State so it has no real connection with these great issues. What matters for the unthinking, as always, is what is immediately enjoyable, and for the thinking, is that one should be true to one's own personality. There will, therefore, be occasions when sexual freedom, public nudity, or cannabis will seem right to express one's feelings, or enlarge one's perceptions.

There will always be those who say wryly that all this was true in a previous generation. The anti-war movements of the thirties and the fight for social justice produced precisely the same theorizing, but it did not lead to drug-taking and there was certainly less sexual permissiveness. This is true but the conditions were entirely different. The people involved were not distinguished so sharply by generation. Society then was much less affluent and young people were relatively even less well-off. The young were thus not yet defined as an important target group for marketing purposes and their self consciousness as a self-contained community was unawakened. Above all it had no international sense. Today, young people feel themselves allied with their generation throughout the world. The issues are international as are the heroes and the prophets. In this sense we are faced with a *generation* which is disconnected and which feels itself out of sympathy with other generations. It has created its own morality and it has had the opportunity and the money to do so.

All this is not to lose sight of the fact that permissiveness is fun. It is clearly much more enjoyable and easy to accept the morality of Aleister Crowley's 'do as you will—that is the whole of the law', than to consider the less immediate attractions offered by the traditionalists. In this, of course, the supporters of the permissive have a very strong card. In a society where promiscuity was frowned upon and the opportunities limited, then everything conspired to defeat the natural wishes of the young. In a disconnected society where promiscuity is obviously practised and where there are plenty of opportunities, everything encourages the fulfilment of natural desire. It is therefore clear that a good deal of the new morality is merely the joyous acceptance of available opportunity, uncomplicated by any but the most superficial rationale. That such an acceptance is possible is also the result of improved methods of birth control, removing the one real fear which promiscuity engendered, and the coming of affluence which enables people to purchase drugs, even when their price is artificially increased by their illegality.

Thus we have a self-conscious society which has the financial ability and the opportunity to decide for itself what its morality shall be. Its virtues are those of variety and excitement and vice is externalized upon the great issues of race, war and poverty for which an earlier generation is responsible.

Two other influences must also be noted. The first is the change in the position of women which has been wrought by the fight for equality. Sexually this has been fundamental. The modesty of the young woman has been a continuous feature of the mores of Western society. It was the leisured classes who set the example in social mores; these women largely lived at home until marriage and by presenting themselves as attractively as possible and playing reasonably hard to get, they caught their man. Perhaps Charlotte Lucas in *Pride and Prejudice* draws the conventional picture most clearly. She says of love: 'We can all *begin* freely—a slight preference is natural enough; but there are very few of us who have heart enough to be really in love without encouragement. In nine cases out of ten, a woman had better show *more* affection than she feels. Bingley likes your sister undoubtedly; but he may never do more than like her, if she does not help him on.' She was, however, clearly to help him on to marriage and any other intention was seriously to her disadvantage. Apart from the obvious danger of having a baby, she would be socially and financially at sea were she to contract any other kind of liaison.

In the twentieth century, the coming of artificial birth control and the economic independence of women has shattered this conventional pattern. Marriage is no longer as essential for woman as it once was. She, like her brothers, is much more

independent of her home and family and she even feels less
responsible for the welfare of aged parents as the community
takes over more of that rôle. It is to this increasingly independent
person that the sexologists and sociologists say, 'you are not
naturally the passive partner in a love affair. It is just as natural
for you to want sex as anyone else.' Thus instead of the former
situation where the boy was expected to say please and the girl
usually answered no, today the girl may well set the pace. All
the pressures upon her are to do precisely that. She is continually told that she too is a sexual animal and that love-making is
a partnership in which she must be fully responsive. It is hardly
surprising that she does not confine her acceptance of this good
advice to the marriage-bed. The whole concept of courtship
and capture has been widely broken down and, whether admirable or not, the last impediment to sexual permissiveness
removed. Both partners are willing and neither need fear an
unwanted child.

Not of course that this has satisfied the extreme feminists.
The emergence of the Women's Liberation Movement in the
U.S.A. and its counterpart in Britain is another example
of a group who, seeing the emptiness of their lives, seek to
blame it on the circumstances of life. The 'burn your bra'
brigade has latched on to the genuine grievance that there is
still much prejudice in the world against the right of women to
take an equal and similar place to men in society. The pace of
change has not been as fast as Germaine Greer and her American counterpart, Betty Frieden, would like but it would
be a pity to foist the majority of women with the kind of
extreme programme of reform which these company sergeant-
majors of the 'monstrous regiment' would like.

Similarly, women are increasingly able to be equal partners
in this disconnected society. Their independence and their
demand for equality make it just as possible for them to join in
the permissive society as the men. In previous generations,
young women were separated from young men, not just for
sexual reasons but because their interests and their opportunities were different. Mixed youth clubs are a relatively new
feature and previously the division between Scouts and Guides
was paralleled in every organization from the Girls' Friendly
Society to the Y.M.C.A. Women looked forward to a different

C

pattern of life from men. They were much more closely tied to their families and their chances of economic independence were much more limited. They tended to have fewer educational opportunities and almost certainly would have considered education to be much less important. Among the upper classes they might be accomplished but their accomplishments would be domestic rather than public. Altogether there would be little chance of a 'disconnected' generation which would embrace both sexes. The generation gap could only become a great divide when young people of both sexes had the independence and opportunity to make up their own minds about morality and live in their own community.

It is clear, therefore, how the permissive society has been able to arise. We can take for granted the natural willingness of the young to be permissive. It is part of their function in the renewal of society in every generation to question every standard and demand the freedom which their natures desire. What has made the use of this freedom possible are the economic and social changes which have at one and the same time given to the young an unheard of independence and economic importance. It follows from this that we cannot see the permissive society as a passing phase, a mere swing of the pendulum. It is the present reaction to a whole new social picture which is common to the Western world but particularly marked in those countries where affluence has made its greatest impact. The attitudes which have been created have been seized upon by many of an older generation—particularly by those with a vested interest in the overthrow of the old order or in being seen to be in tune with the demands of the young. Curiously enough the Communists have failed to make much headway in this saga. Their attitude towards society with its concept of the class war and the creation of the socialist state is all too obviously conservative for the proponents of change. It has been the believers in continuous change who have benefited most. Maoists, Trotskyites and the followers of Marcuse have a common approach to order which must be most attractive to those for whom variety and excitement are so important. Order to them is violent and essentially uncreative. It is only in the throes of continuous revolution that man can be creative. This is, of course, an attitude which is held only by a very small minority on the fringes of the great mass of young people but it is an attitude which has far-reaching effects and to which I will return later.

In the meantime, the changes among the young have been welcomed by all the ageing remnants of the pre-war Left. The public issues which the students have espoused are dear to their hearts and the horror which long-haired youth has aroused among the conventional middle-class is heaven indeed to an intellectual Socialist in decline. No wonder that all the left-wing publishers of Europe and America have been atwitter preparing their books on student revolt and producing the far more profitable shocking novels and plays which demonstrate the freedom which the new attitudes have won for them. The Grove Press in America has skilfully linked popular pornography with the radical views of the young. 'Do you have what it takes to join the underground?' says the advertising insert in the middle of its reprint of the Victorian erotic magazine *The Pearl*. If your answer is yes then you mail off an application form which begins 'Gentlemen: I am adventurous, literate, adult and wish to take advantage of your offer. . . .' You can then select two free titles from a list of books published by the firm which 'provides a platform for the best of the new writing and art'. The titles are illuminating—*My Secret Life*, the remarkable, erotic Victorian autobiography; *Harriet Marwood, Governess*—the story of the 'education' of a young man by his beautiful but depraved Victorian governess; *120 days of Sodom*—by the Marquis de Sade; *The Olympia Reader*—with special emphasis on material never before published in the U.S.; *The Story of O*; Aubrey Beardsley's *Selected Drawings*—by one of the greatest decadents of the nineties; De Sade's *Justine* together with one of his most daring works, *Philosophy in the Bedroom*. Lastly you can choose a three-in-one selection: *Call me Brick*—a fast-reading, hilarious, contemporary novel about an impatient and uninhibited young girl's initiation into adult relationships; *Sadopaideia*, an anonymous work of fiction which details the experiences of an Oxford undergraduate, 'showing how he was led through the pleasant paths of masochism to the supreme joys of sadism'; and *4 × 4* a volume which combines four extraordinary first novels by four young American writers who concern themselves with various sexual adventures and misadventures.

We shall discuss later the close connection between pornography and the radical movement, but what is absolutely clear is that drug-culture, pornography, and extreme radicalism are usually found together—and nowhere so obviously as in the world of publishing. There the cry of 'Freedom!' goes up immediately any attack is made on any obscene publication. It is, of course, very important for the leftover Left to find a new way of fitting the new student radical into their world view. For this, the concept of their fighting for freedom of expression is quite useful and enables publishers to link together the radical views and the obscenities which are calculated to annoy the forces of order.

Thus just as the permissive society has been brought about by the whole change in the position of the young, it has been given an extreme rationale by the radical Left, and it has been welcomed by that part of the Lilac Establishment which thinks that it is merely a stage in the creation of the tolerant society. John Calder, Joint Secretary of the Defence of Literature and the Arts Society and publisher of *Last Exit to Brooklyn* has summed this attitude up succinctly:

'Society has changed and will change again, not back to the cosy middle-class paradise of forty years ago, but forward, either to a violent society in which no value will be safe and no person, or if we tackle the problem of violence now with intelligent social engineering, possibly a truly liberal and tolerant society that cares for everyone and their problems and gives every child a schooling for life that will enable him to understand the world intelligently, to live in it happily, and play a full part in building that society.'

What a lovely, good thought that is. Rather a long way from 'the pleasant paths of masochism and the supreme joys of sadism'; not entirely in tune with drug-crazed killings by hippy 'families'; and possibly more attainable in a society with deeper values than those of variety and excitement—but still a lovely, good thought.

It certainly serves to point to the wide range of those who advocate the permissive society. There is the traditional support from men like Calder who really want the permissive society because they believe that it was previously a privilege 'for those inside the right circles but never to be allowed to the great unwashed outside'. They want it because it provides a sort of equality of opportunity in vice. Then there is the broad mass of young people who have had the opportunity to create it. Beyond them both are the apostles of disorder for whom permissiveness in sex and drugs is merely part of a new permissiveness which would replace order with continual revolution and bring us to 'a violent society in which no value will be safe and no person'.

We have then a motley collection of supporters. Their motives range from a real frustration with a society which restricts their freedom in ways which they feel deeply; to a desire to overthrow that society altogether. So, just as we found the nature of the permissive society much more complex than is usually thought, so too its genesis and its supporters are variegated in the extreme. It is therefore not surprising that the reactions of the authorities —both of Church and State—have been similarly diverse.

3 Life

The coming of the permissive society in legislative terms has been a piecemeal operation. The attitudes of the intellectual élite have been marked by their uncompromising support for the principle of individual freedom. They have therefore been unaffected by any real understanding of the importance of community living and of that delicate balance which maintains a society built up since classical times.

Society is an organic structure whose parts are linked in the most complicated fashion. A community like ours cannot easily take out a strand in the complex web of related laws and conventions which govern it, no one of which can be treated in isolation but all of which go to make up a pattern of relationships which serve both to protect the individual and to preserve the community.

The arguments of those who would extend the permissive society fall into two categories. There are the few, but the influential few, who would change our society totally; those who, like Dr Edmund Leach, would change its basis by 'abolishing' the family or, who like Jerry Rubin, replace political democracy by some anarchic system. The majority, however, are more modest in their aims and would just like to be free of some of the restraints in society which they feel are onerous. They, like John Calder, claim to respect the ends of civilization but dispute the present means. They would sweep away the restrictions which they see as frustrations in order to achieve civilizations's real purposes. They agree with the traditionalists in seeing violence as the potential destroyer but find that violence cannot be contained within the traditional forms. They see as the only hope the removal of restraints which society places unnecessarily upon its members so that these restraints do not engender the frustration which will lead to its overthrow. So it is not that they present us with an alternative society, fundamentally different and yet as valid as the present one.

It is merely that these moderates urge piecemeal change of our laws and attitudes in order to protect the fundamental values of our civilization. What we have to decide is whether traditional society can withstand these changes which, viewed by themselves may be perfectly fitting, but seen in context may undermine the basic structure. The issue is rarely one of isolated principle but much more often a matter of judgment within the total situation.

Lord Devlin is right when he suggests that a lawmaker does not have to decide whether a proposition can be defended in absolute terms but whether it is right in the circumstances of the society with which he is concerned. Thus he does not have to take into account whether in essence polygamy is inferior to monogamy, all he need do is decide that in western society, monogamy is an essential part of our structure and that until such time as we decide fundamentally to alter that structure, it is reasonable and right for society to protect its interests as a community by legally defining and defending monogamy. It is not that we have to be able to justify such a legal position philosophically and for all time; it is merely that we have to prove that it has become so central to the organization of our community that its removal would be destructive of our whole way of life. Of course if there were to come a time when the entire community was so convinced of the need for a change that it was willing and able to refashion itself throughout then we might start taking more than one husband or wife. Monogamy may have been instituted because of Christianity but it has been retained because it has become part and parcel of the structure of our community.

It is thus important that we do not approach any of the basic attitudes of law or convention too glibly. It is not a conclusive argument that the original beliefs that gave rise to these attitudes are no longer held; they must instead be seen as part of the whole pattern which makes up our civilization. It is not that the pattern may not with advantage be changed; it is just that change can rarely be isolated as conveniently as fashion would like.

When we come to look at the institutions which are based on the concept of the sanctity of human life, we face these problems in their most acute and vital form. Our society is based ultimately upon this essential value—a value which is independent of the quality of the individual or his use to the community but which is intrinsic. This is a truth which some hold as self-evident. We may be perfectly aware that it is in fact a result of our Christian inheritance but we cannot throw it aside merely because we have ceased to take for granted the truth of the Gospels. It is, after all, an assumption which is basic to the civilization which we have sought to build and is recognized as such in the formularies of the United Nations. It has a continuing validity unconnected with its religious basis—a validity as the underlying assumption from which all our attitudes to equality, tolerance, and freedom flow. It is this realization which has engendered the fervour of so many who have fought for the abolition of capital punishment. It is not that they have seen the criminal as especially deserving of their campaign but that they have had so clear an appreciation of the sacredness of human life that they have had a vital interest in the State's power over lives, even of murderers. If the death penalty does not save innocent lives, they say, then it must not be used, however inconvenient the alternatives. This has nothing to do with the value of the murderer to the community or the quality of his life but is concerned with the value the community puts on all life. The fact that the assumption that all human life is sacred is based on the religious belief, that all men are precious in the sight of God, their Creator, cannot invalidate it in the eyes of the non-believer. It has become a prerequisite for the continuance of civilization and must be accepted as such by the community.

Opposition to the Nazi concept that racial considerations override the sanctity of human life, or the Communist belief that economic interests may do likewise, may be impossible without some adherence to the divine sanction implicit in the Christian belief in the fatherhood of God and the brotherhood of man. It is, however, perfectly possible for a society to say that the sanctity of human life is so important a part of the structure of that society that it must be protected and defended by law and custom and that against this, neither convenience nor reasons of state may prevail.

This is of course a very inconvenient principle for the permissive society. It puts individualism in jeopardy at three very sensitive points. It questions a man's right to take his own life, his right to take away the life that he has created, and his right to ask another to take his life. Suicide, abortion, and euthanasia —all perfectly permissible according to the individualist creed—become matters of great seriousness when looked at in the context of the society which we have created.

The question of suicide throws this into relief most effectively because there is fair unanimity that legal restraints are ineffectual. The question thus resolves itself into whether the community ought to discourage it and on what grounds. For the Christian community there was really not much argument. The appeal to Scripture said 'Thou shalt not kill'; reason called suicide irresponsible; the Church pointed to it as removing the possibility of repentance; and the conscience counted it cowardly. For today's rational man it is not so clear. His reason tells him that the man without ties may commit suicide responsibly and his conscience tells him that the act may be braver than to live. Yet if we kill ourselves we do, in the popular phrase, 'say no to life'. We deny that human life is sacred. As G. K. Chesterton emphasizes: 'The man who kills himself kills all men; as far as he is concerned he wipes out the world.' We have a duty to the community to affirm the value of life, it is a basic duty which overrides our individual feelings or beliefs. It does so because without the acceptance of that basic truth *our* community could not function. Another community might —it is possible to envisage a society in which human life is not accorded an intrinsic value. It might be a very nasty society but not an impossible one. What is more important is that it is not *our* society. As its life is dependent upon the acceptance of the sanctity of all life, then it can and should demand of its members this acceptance, whether or not they believe in the Christian God.

If then society has a right to ask its members to abstain from self-murder does this necessarily mean that it must make such an action illegal? Suicide is illegal in most European countries but not in Britain or most American states. Before 1961, the attempted suicide had rarely been brought to court in Britain but his treatment was so inconsistent as to be scandalous, and the abolition was designed to put an end to this. In New York, suicide is not illegal but it is stigmatized by society. In both cases governments have seen that the law does little to reduce the incidence of suicide and may indeed encourage the victim to make sure he does a good job. This is particularly dangerous as it is increasingly clear that suicide is often the last despairing plea for help rather than an actual decision to take one's life. Thus, just as the community should refuse people the right to take their own lives, it has a duty to see that every help is available for those who attempt to do so. Making suicide illegal does inhibit people from seeking help when in desperation they decide to act and it makes help more difficult to obtain if the attempt has been foiled, for relations and friends do not wish to risk the chance that the victim may be prosecuted.

The absence of British suicide laws has meant that the authorities are unable to enter premises where a suicide is suspected because no crime is being committed. It does also seem that, if the community really has learnt the lesson of the Nazis and the Communists, it ought to make its position clear on the value of life. Both conditions could be fulfilled if suicide was still a crime but one which did not involve prosecution. This would give the police a *locus standi* which they would otherwise not have and enable the community to take cognizance of attempted suicides so that help could be channelled to them.

Of course this runs counter to the views of those who talk more enthusiastically than accurately of the honourable suicides of Greece and Rome. Apart from the detail that most of these suicides were punished in Greece and many in Rome, this view ignores the fact that we do not actually live in the Graeco-Roman world. We do not permit slavery. We have a totally different view of the proper restrictions of power—all because we have a different attitude to the value of human life. The simple assertion that in other societies men found it perfectly possible to do things which our society has found it necessary to condemn may be no more valid than to say different societies are different. It is a requirement of the kind of society which we have established that the sanctity of human life be accepted as a fundamental tenet. Other societies with different values and habits may not have that requirement but that is no reason for suggesting that we are therefore absolved from any necessity to retain it, still less for arguing that the State has no right to proceed with laws which assume that such a view ought to be held.

Yet there is of course a sense in which suicide is not a crucial matter. There is no sign that it is becoming an epidemic, although the rate is rising steadily in Western European countries and the problem cannot be ignored. Where we really have to come up against the terrifying facts is when considering abortion.

Abortion is an activity to which only the affluent societies seem addicted. No society before the present one has aborted on any large scale and even we have only begun to do so over the past three or four decades. This cannot be because abortion has suddenly become much safer; Western society has practised it even where it is illegal and can largely be done only by the amateur methods. Naturally this is not to say that there has not been *any* abortion before the present century. Yet, although one can point to times when child exposure was accepted, or others when mutilation of the male genitals provided a sort of birth control, in no society before our own can abortion be seen as a regular practice. And regular practice it certainly is, even if we take the lowest estimates of illegal abortions. Before the legislation changed Sweden had 20,000 criminal abortions a year, today with a more liberal abortion code which allows State abortions on medical, social, and humanitarian grounds, the estimate for illegal abortions is even higher. In Japan where abortion was available almost on demand, the notified abortions in 1964 were one million, with a likely one million unreported in a population of under 98 million. In Britain, before abortion was widely allowed, estimates varied between 10,000 and 100,000 illegal abortions every year. Similar figures have been produced for every developed country.

It does therefore seem to be true that despite safer contraception, abortion is still a problem. Women who use birth control methods are psychologically so unprepared for child-bearing that they are often totally unwilling to accept that they have conceived. We take for granted that we can decide whether we wish a child or not and we are quite determined to insist upon that right.

The second factor which has made abortion so much more prevalent has been the escalation of material expectation. Affluence has predisposed parents to expect more as a minimum standard of life for themselves and for their children. They are thus even more unwilling than before to bring a child into the world unless they feel that they can give it what they consider to be a proper start in life. They are also increasingly unwilling to accept the cut in their own standard of life which the arrival of a new baby may mean. Thus, through a mixture of selfishness and the proper regard for the future of the child, parents are determined that no mistake shall upset their plans.

The third reason for this growth in abortion is that people are now undoubtedly more sexually permissive. The arrival of artificial contraception has meant that many have seen no reason why they should not sleep around, with a consequent increase in the number of children conceived either through the failure of a contraceptive device or because one was not used by a couple who would normally do so. The effect is particularly marked among middle-class girls who are earning their own living and who therefore have neither the wish to have a baby nor the need to get married in order to legitimize it. These are precisely the girls who are not prepared to accept the principle of the shotgun wedding even if the man agrees. In the same circumstances the man is just as likely to deny all responsibility on the grounds that the girl can perfectly well look after herself now that the Pill is widely available. In such circumstances, abortion whether illegal or legal is sought.

Now the pro-abortionists who have lately scored two notable victories—the first in Great Britain and the second in New York —argue that there is nothing that we can do about this situation and that therefore we may as well accept it as part of our lives at least until there is a completely reliable contraceptive. This kind of cheap attitude to the issue is enough to drive one to the most extreme position so that we almost wish that methods of contraception had never been invented. It is an attitude which certainly makes understandable the Roman Catholic view on birth control even if it does not vindicate it. It does seem perfectly true, as Pope Pius XII warned, that the coming of birth control has changed our whole attitude towards sex. It is not just that we have rightly thrown out the concept that its only real purpose was to have babies; it is that we have swung to the opposite extreme and now act as if we believe that its only purpose is to have fun *without* having babies.

Up to the twentieth century, no society practised abortion widely, and all Western societies condemned and punished it. In the last few years, however, certain countries have allowed abortion, although there is a tendency to tighten up the laws after a few years of liberalization. In Japan, legal abortion meant that their net reproduction rate fell to the lowest in the world and, instead of being worried about overpopulation, they faced a frightening imbalance between the old and the young. Russia allowed abortion from 1920 to 1936 and then banned it except for strong medical reasons. Hungary and Czechoslovakia both allow it under tough safeguards. Hawaii has abortion practically on demand. Sweden has made it fairly freely available and there has also been an increase in illegal abortions. In France there are enormous numbers of illegal abortions with some estimates being as high as 400,000 a year. All such figures are perforce estimates. They are often inaccurate, though often used to press the legalization case. The U.K. newspaper, the *Guardian*, headlines the researches of a lady from Berkeley who claimed that Italy had 4,000 illegal abortions a day! That makes $1\frac{1}{2}$ million abortions a year in a population of 54 million! The report went on to allege 'several hundred' mothers a day died from abortion. That would make the death rate at least 110,000 a year out of a total death rate of 530,000. Now supposing that half the people who die in Italy are males this figure would suggest that 40% of females who die, die from illegal abortion—a rather unlikely figure. But then so is the idea of $1\frac{1}{2}$ million abortions a year—that is eight times the British figure where abortion is usually legal! Given that the Italians also have nearly one million live births it argues an unparalleled degree of fecundity! This ought to serve as a warning of the inaccuracy of the statistics quoted and upon which we have to make our judgements.

It is in this situation that we have to assess the effect of continually improving methods of contraception, the growing realization that overpopulation is a major hazard, and the fact that the pressure for legal abortion will continue. Clearly, where contraception is not freely available but where all the other elements which encourage a more permissive attitude to sex are present, the number of illegal abortions will be very high. It is perfectly true that knowledge about birth control is essential if there is to be any chance of limiting the incidence of abortion.

What is, however, also clear is that contraception does not appear to have any effect on the reproductive pattern obtaining in a nation whereas abortion does. As the Japanese expert, Dr Yowhio Koya, said to the World Population Congress in Belgrade in 1965: 'If people at large were once accustomed to induced abortion, it might be extremely difficult to make them come back to the previous reproductive behaviour.' This has certainly been the experience of Japan which has had the greatest period of abortion being freely available and it would be particularly dangerous in the Western world where many countries, like Sweden, are already worried about their low birth rates.

We are then faced with the most remarkable series of paradoxes. At a time in history when man finds birth control easier than ever before, he has the greatest pressure for allowing abortion on demand. At a time when Western man is richer than ever before he is most concerned to stop pregnancies for financial reasons. At a time when all reasons would seem to dictate the contrary, mankind is faced with the problem of widespread legal and illegal abortion—a problem which has never faced him in any major way before. How curious too, that at exactly the point when we have begun to break down the stigma of illegitimacy and when all Western countries are making every effort to provide for the unmarried mother and her child, we decide that it is essential for unwanted pregnancies to be terminated.

Terminated—what a good word. Civilization always finds a euphemism for that which it would prefer not to discuss. A mother who is looking forward to the birth refers to her 'child'; one for whom it is a nuisance calls it a 'foetus'. 'Terminating the pregnancy' or 'removing the foetus' are so much more acceptable than 'killing the baby'. Yet no description of abortion can be more accurate than this last. It is of course true that Aristotelian biology suggested that the baby passed from a lower form of life into its human form about the fortieth or the eightieth day, depending on whether it were a boy or a girl. No such milestone can be discerned in the progress of the child from conception and nidation to birth. One might argue that the life of the baby only becomes a fact when the fertilized egg implants itself in the womb—which it does within the first week. It is quite plausible to suggest that many fertilized ova are expelled naturally up to that point, but that life begins when the new potential in the embryo settles down to grow. This obviously would be of importance in any discussion of an *ex post facto* birth control pill. One cannot deny thereafter there is no time in the growth of the child when the infant is not alive. True it cannot exist on its own but nor can a premature baby who depends upon an oxygen tent for life. We cannot even fix a date for the point at which it can exist on its own. All we can say is that this is a life and, barring an induced abortion, it will be practically certain to be born alive. Can then a civilization, whose cardinal principle is the sanctity of human life, accept that hundreds of thousands of women every year will queue up, with the blessing of the law, to have the life within them destroyed, often for no better reason than that it is inconvenient? What a total denial of human values and human instincts that is. The mother takes it upon herself that the child shall not be born. She may cite one of the notorious 'social' reasons in the British Act, which will allow her almost any latitude to get an abortion. She may arrange her abortion through one of the clinics where not too many questions are asked nor too searching an examination given. The real reason in many cases is that she does not want the baby. It may be because she is unmarried, or because she already has enough children and this was a mistake. It may be because she does not want a child yet or that she fancies herself too poor for one. These are excellent reasons but they are reasons for using birth control methods.

Even the most fervent supporter of abortion will admit that the child is really alive just before birth and will limit abortion to the first sixteen or at most twenty-four weeks of pregnancy. Yet what really changes in the seventeenth or twenty-fifth week? Merely the fact that even those with the hardest hearts and weakest heads begin to feel squeamish when fully-formed children, able to cry, are thrown into the incinerator. It is particularly interesting that people who are quite willing to support abortion in principle get very upset when the operation is put in these terms. They accuse one of emotion but their accusation is that the reality of killing the baby has been allowed to break through the antiseptic illusion of 'terminating' the pregnancy. As long as the child does not look too much like a child, as long as the child can be discussed as a foetus, so long are the extreme pro-abortionists happy.

Nor would there be any reason to be as blunt about it were it not that the reformists refuse to face the issue. For them the heart must only go out to the mother and they cite, quite properly, all the terrible circumstances which may arise and in which abortion may seem the better choice between evils. It is precisely because we must face up to these exceptional cases with all the compassion that is in us, that we must distinguish them from the usual run-of-the-mill abortion. Only a tiny minority of those who seek an abortion can really be said to be in such trouble that life or sanity depend on the destruction of the baby. Instead, for most, abortion does later what birth control was meant to have done earlier. The only difference being that one *prevents* an unwanted life and the other *destroys* it. This is the crucial difference. Man is often faced with distinguishing between what *might* be and what *is*, and he is as often concerned to confuse the issue.

It does seem then that abortion is clearly not desirable except for the gravest of reasons. It appears to be one of those problems which arise only in an affluent society and, legal or illegal, it is a major issue in every Western country. Where the law is strict but still allows abortion in some cases it has the effect of encouraging illegal abortion by giving a sufficient sanction to the principle to mitigate society's disapproval but not enough laxity to enable all so encouraged to get one legally. Where abortion is freely available it discourages the spread of contraception, may have permanent effects on reproduction patterns, and breaches the State's commitment to the up-holding of the sanctity of human life and the protection of those who cannot protect themselves. It also means that the State which operates a free welfare system has some crucial decisions to make about the extent of the medical resources which it is prepared to devote to cosmetic abortions. This last is by no means unimportant. In Britain there are long queues of women waiting for operations without which they will continue to live in pain. Yet beds in National Health hospitals which they could have occupied are being used for the 84,000 abortions which were done from the coming into force of the Act up to October 1970. Abortions, by their very nature, have to be done at once and their legalization has had the effect of changing the priorities within the National Health system so that resources have been diverted without any real consideration of the justification. Even where the cost of the abortion is borne by the mother, as in the U.S.A., in many European countries and in two-thirds of British abortions, the allocation of scarce medical resources to this purpose must itself pose practical problems.

What is certainly true is that the operation of the law in Great Britain and in New York State has resulted in some very disturbing evidence. There appear to be a significant number of women who return for second and third abortions after only a few months. Many of these are married women and seem to have been pressurized into the operation by husbands who did not want the added financial burden. They themselves would often like to have a child and it is the subconscious recognition of this that leads them continually to conceive despite their husbands' opposition.

It is, of course, also true that countries with more 'liberal' laws become magnets for women who want a cosmetic abortion. The private clinics in London, with their commission to taxi drivers who bring pregnant women to them, their special terms for unmarried foreign girls, their lack of aftercare, and the enormous profits—these are the incidental effects of the changes in the law. It is not therefore surprising that 256 members of the House of Commons signed a motion demanding a thorough investigation into the workings of the Abortion Act only two years after it had been passed and that the Ministry of Social Security has had to set up that enquiry. Not least among the reasons which made the investigation timely was the growing evidence that the incidence of illegal abortions, even in a country with so few restrictions, was as high as it had been before the passing of the Act.

What then of the exceptions: the child who endangers the mother's life; the child who is conceived as a result of rape; the child who may be deformed. In England, before the recent liberalizing Act, the first two were thought to be allowable as a result of the Bourne judgment. This was a matter of case law

D

and had not properly been defined. In practice, if not in strict accordance with the law, such abortions are carried out in most Western nations. It would seem reasonable that the State should give doctors the right to abort if it will save the life of the mother. This is not to transgress the ultimate sanctity of human life, it is not to destroy life needlessly, and, unlike other abortions, it does not destroy the doctor's unique purpose of seeking in all possible ways to save life. The question of a child conceived as a result of rape is in fact a very rare one indeed. There would be a great increase in the number of so-called rapes if this were made one of a limited number of grounds upon which abortion should be procurable. In any case it is difficult, even in the very small number of true cases, to say that the child should be killed, unless of course it is seriously endangering the life of the mother. Like any other child the offspring of the attack is growing inside the mother. It did not ask to be born, but then neither did any of us. It is a life against which the only objection is the manner of its fathering— and that is an objection which in these enlightened times we should be hard put to defend in accordance with our views on equality of opportunity, classlessness, and racial understanding.

It is sometimes suggested that this is an intolerable imposition upon the mother—she has been violated once, now she is to be violated for a further period while her body is host to a child she never wanted. There is no doubt that this is a terrible imposition. The mother must go through all the months of pregnancy with none of the joy of expectation to sustain her, none of the support of a husband who loved her, and none of the pleasure of knowing that she carried a child she had conceived in that love. It is indeed an imposition. Yet is it so intolerable an imposition that we must kill in order to remove it? Must the State give up its duty to protect the innocent, or should we instead ask our citizens to pay the cost of a society where human life is valued utterly. That society must then do everything possible to help the mother concerned for she is witnessing to the value of life on behalf of the community. Perhaps this is the real meaning of 'all you need is love'—love for those whom you cannot like. Yes it is an imposition, but it is one which we are bound to bear. Blindness and deafness are also impositions but we know well that it is when the blind and the deaf seek to overcome those impositions that the truly human qualities are seen.

What then of the deformed child? The first thought in almost every parent's mind on the birth of a child is—'Is he all right?' The thalidomide cases brought this situation to a head. Can we really justify bearing a child whom we know will probably be deformed? The effect of German measles on the pregnant woman seems even more terrifying; at least with thalidomide there was a 75 per cent chance that the child would be normal. German measles contracted in the first three months of pregnancy means little hope of a normal baby.

Yet we must separate fact from emotion and face up to the result. There are very few cases indeed in which it can be 100 per cent certain that a child will be abnormal and even fewer where the degree of abnormality can be forecast. Therefore, for the majority of abortions on this ground, we shall kill the baby *in case*. For these, as for the much smaller group of those whom we *know* will be abnormal, we have to ask what degree of abnormality is sufficient to make death preferable to life. Here we really are in an impossible situation. We can say that the child which has no brain, which will not survive more than a few days, and can be detected before birth, can with reason be aborted for it will not live. There are certain other extreme situations where the child is incapable of any kind of human relationship and is in fact a 'monster', unable to live long. Abortion here is obviously acceptable. But what of the rest. Surely we do not have the right to decide that a child would prefer to die than live deformed. Any study of the handicapped will show that almost every single one of them would prefer to have been born.

In opposition to this people say that the baby in the womb does not know and therefore cannot make the choice and it is no hardship for it to be denied what it has never known. In lesser matters this argument would be unacceptable. We do not deny the child the right to learn history on the grounds that at that point he knows no history and therefore cannot know what he is missing. We say instead that he does not know *now* but he *will* know and on the best evidence we have he will prefer to have been educated. We therefore make education compulsory although we are aware that there will be some who will say at the end of it that they wish they had been allowed to wander free as air.

Can we not say the same thing about the child in the womb? He does not know what life in the world will be like and we therefore have to make a choice for him. That choice must be based upon the best of our knowledge, our duty towards him, our duty towards the community in which he could live, and our duty towards the family which will bring him up. It is our duty towards the community to safeguard human life; to the best of our knowledge we would choose life rather than death, to the best of our ability the community ought to provide help to the family of the child—either by relieving it of the duty to care for the child or by making every aid available to those who wish to care for it at home. As human beings we can make only one choice—we cannot kill the child.

Now there are two other arguments which have to be faced here. The first is that used by the women who campaign for abortion. They say that men cannot discuss the matter. They do not have babies and therefore they 'do not know'. This argument has the same force as that of the racialist who says to a liberal that he may not discuss the policies of the South African Government because he has not been to South Africa. Or of the Communist who says that only by residence in the German Democratic Republic can one understand its joys. The person whose comments have been discounted can answer reasonably in both cases that the man who has lived in either country has a very special testimony to offer. He will certainly be better informed but it may be that he will also be less objective. That must be judged on the evidence he produces.

The same is true of the abortion argument. Women have a special rôle to play in the discussion but it does not make them the only people qualified to talk about the issue. The sanctity of human life, like the freedom involved in the two parallel examples, is an issue which concerns the *whole* community. It also vitally concerns the child, about whose rights the woman is no more qualified to argue than any man.

The other case put forward is that based upon convenience. It says that it is wrong to bring into the world children who are going to be a drain on society and that society has a right to refuse the burden and destroy the child. This argument we shall encounter again when we discuss euthanasia. It is usually presented more attractively from the point of view of the child. Is it fair, people ask, to bring such a child into the world, when you know it will spend its life in institutions—a burden to itself and others? This concept begs every possible question. It assumes that we bring the child into the world at birth rather than at conception—a view which, although enormously convenient, just is not tenable. It then suggests that you *know* it will be deformed, which, as we have seen, you very rarely do. Finally, and here is the crunch, it brings the question of the burden upon others into the argument. Both the previous assumptions are really induced by the desire to get rid of this child because he is inconvenient and expensive. So often this is an important factor in the demand of the woman who wishes to have an abortion, although not usually stated in these terms. In either case—whether the argument be from the point of view of the mother or of society—we cannot kill because the life is inconvenient, even if it is desperately so. The community must accept the cost of providing for unwanted children because it is the price of protecting life.

It is important in these arguments to talk about human beings without concern for their quality. The whole point of the sanctity of human life is that it applies to all—whether they be great minds or not, whether they make a major contribution to society, are rich and successful or whether they are poor and a burden on the State. There may be other rights which a properly constituted community would insist upon adding to this but this is the *basic* right. For this reason we have not discussed famous men and women who might have been aborted in the past had our attitude then obtained. The issue is not what the world would lose or what the world would gain, it is what society would imperil by denying the basic right to life to those whose only protection is the community.

Nevertheless, as we have discussed the objection that the community has such a heavy burden to bear in looking after the handicapped, it is worth remembering that under the law of England or New York as it now stands, Helen Keller would have been aborted. Even more compelling perhaps is the conversation between two doctors which Maurice Baring used to quote and which Norman St John Stevas cites in his book *The*

Right to Life. 'One doctor said to another, "About the terminating of a pregnancy, I want your opinion. The father was syphillitic. The mother was tuberculous. Of the four children born, the first was blind, the second died, the third was deaf, the fourth also tuberculous. What would you have done?" "I should have ended the pregnancy," said the other. "Then you would have murdered Beethoven." '

This story may be melodramatic but nevertheless it has its point. We cannot make a decision about the life of a baby, precisely because we can never be in full possession of the facts. We certainly cannot tell whether his deformity will be such that he will be a drain on the community or such that in rising above it he will make a major contribution to the community.

The story also rings true in one other respect. The doctor who is for the abortion says 'I should have ended the pregnancy' and, while we are thinking of the baby as a foetus, that seems perfectly proper. The other doctor then says 'You would have murdered Beethoven', and then, when we are thinking of the foetus as a child, that seems perfectly proper. Is it not true that we know perfectly well that we cannot distinguish adequately between the claims of the unborn child and the child already born? We are therefore thrust back upon the expedient of using a euphemism to protect us in our difficulty. We know that we must think of the child in the womb as if it had no future, yet we also know that this is not the way the mother usually thinks of her pregnancy. 'When I was having you,' she says to her child, talking of the early months of pregnancy. She is in no doubt that the foetus is a child and thereby shows practically what we know theoretically—that there can only be a formal distinction between that which is to be born and that which has been born.

There are those who believe that even after birth the community should be prepared to decide that a particular life is likely to be so deprived that it is better to take it away. This disposes of the difficulty presented by abortion which takes place at a time when it is impossible to tell whether the baby is deformed or not. Logically there ought to be no difficulty for the abortionist. He ought to say that the child has no experience of life, it has no chance of remaining alive except through the mother's care, and if the baby is born deformed then it is perfectly reasonable for the community, which will probably have to care for him, to make up its mind on his behalf whether it is better for him to live or die.

Somehow most people shrink from this. When the arguments are revealed in their starkness and not confused by the clinical terminology of the abortion controversy, few would really suggest that we have a right to decide to kill in these circumstances. Nevertheless the view is gaining ground. The fear occasioned by Hitler's use of the same argument is subsiding and the eugenic concepts which led to the founding of euthanasia campaigns in Britain and America in the 1930s are becoming more acceptable.

It was the case of Mme van der Put, the Belgian accused of killing her thalidomide baby which, by occasioning a great deal of understandable sympathy and even more confusion, brought the euthanasia issue to a head again. Sympathy for the mother is not only natural it is actually an acknowledged part of the law in those countries which, like Great Britain, treat murder of a child by its mother up to one year after birth as a much lesser crime of infanticide. In others it is the practice to commute the charge to one of manslaughter for precisely the same reason— that the mother is under very special stress at that time and cannot be prosecuted under normal terms. At the same time, Mme van der Put, in taking her child's life, abrogated to herself the right to decide whether another human being should live or die. Who is to say what amount of abnormality was enough for such a decision? Her child was terribly deformed, yet its mind was not directly affected. It could have grown up with its senses complete and could have been able to associate with other people. Was she justified in saying that it may not live? Was she, as the mother of a newborn baby, really entirely unselfish in her decision or was it not reasonable to suppose that the problems of rearing such a child did not play some, even subconscious, part? In fact her behaviour is entirely understandable but entirely unacceptable.

We cannot accept that parents can have such power over their children that they shall decide whether they should live or die. But, say the supporters of euthanasia, that is not what we mean; what we want is for such children to be destroyed not solely at the behest of the parents but with the agreement of the doctors concerned or preferably with a certificate from a properly constituted board. After all, it is well known that doctors allow extremely handicapped children to die, why not other severely disabled babies? The fact that this is a polite way of stating the Hitlerian argument, should not condemn it out of hand, but it ought to warn us of the dangers involved. Again the child has no say in the matter. Those who were in this position and who were allowed to live would almost universally opt for life. The principle that murder can be allowed even though life will not be saved is a dangerous one indeed and the idea of keeping the child alive while a board decides if it is to live or not is a barbarous one. In any case the concept of being able to draw up a kind of gruesome list of categories which would enable a child to die or not is surely unacceptable. It is also difficult to see whether the parents should continue to have a say in this. If the community is going to have to care for the baby, are the parents going to be permitted to seek to allow the child to live even though its deformities are such that the community would normally kill it.

All in all, euthanasia of a deformed child is not acceptable. Now for the argument that doctors allow the anencephalic child to die. This usually refers to those children who live only a few days because they are in fact too damaged to survive. The doctor is certainly not obliged to prolong vegetable life by extreme measures in these cases. He need not use extraordinary means to continue the breathing which under any other circumstances would stop.

This last is also true of the prolongation of life of the old where, by taking extraordinary methods, life can be perpetuated with no hope of any improvement. In such a case the old should be allowed to die in peace. We should not be so imprisoned by the advances in modern drugs that we seek to keep alive as a vegetable someone who would otherwise have died. This does, of course, demand of the doctor a great responsibility but one which is inherent in modern medical advances. The advocates of euthanasia would like the old and the chronically ill to have the right to ask for their death. Many who would agree that the baby who cannot consent to his death must be saved, would suggest that it is perfectly acceptable for someone to opt for euthanasia.

This is much the most difficult case to discuss because it is really suicide by another's hand. It is the request of someone who cannot commit suicide that another should do it for him. Very often the appeal is put in the enormously emotional terms of old people in great pain wanting merely to be put out of their agony. It ought therefore to be admitted that the number of such people is very small and estimates of how many people would avail themselves of euthanasia are always extremely low. The advance of modern painkilling drugs is such that it is in the rarest of cases people are in terrible pain which cannot be controlled.

Yet there are other pressures to which old people are subject and which can be very great and must be taken into account. There are those who do not want to feel a burden on others and for whom the distress of relatives can be very saddening. It would be wrong if these people should in a selfless way demand euthanasia, not because of their suffering but because of the pain which they feel they cause to others. Life is too precious to be exposed to this kind of pressure. There is, of course, also the case where the old person is improperly influenced by relatives who wish to be rid of the burden and who transfer their own desires to the mind of the patient. In both cases the euthanasia societies in Britain and America propose very stringent rules and investigation by an independent board. Any such system would, however, frustrate what is evidently the purpose of allowing a person to choose to be killed. It hardly allows him to die peacefully. Nor does it get over the major psychological difficulty which is that we are again introducing into hospitals the possibility that the doctor and the nurse instead of being always concerned with the preservation of life must instead, in certain circumstances, bring death. Anyone who is in contact with old people will know how deep is the suspicion of hospitals for precisely this reason, and anything which may dissuade the ill from entering hospital is surely to be deplored.

Even if we put aside all the arguments against suicide it still seems that euthanasia brings with it such problems of control that it cannot reasonably be allowed. In the case of the incurable patient it is difficult to accept the arguments which are tendered. The complexity involved in defining an incurable disease in these days of rapid medical advance, the problem of facing up to the medical phenomenon of the incurable disease which suddenly halts in its progress, and the other points already raised in the discussion both of euthanasia and of suicide would suggest what appears to be the view of every country in the world except Uruguay—that euthanasia should not be allowed.

This concern for human life has been an element running throughout Judaeo-Christian thought. It has been an essential part of the creation of our Western civilization. It is indeed 'built into the structure of our way of life' as Lord Devlin has recently emphasized. Yet it would seem particularly crucial to us today. It is not just that we have gone through a period in which the activities of the Nazi government in Germany and Communist governments in China and the Soviet Union have shown such scant regard for human life. We must not forget how near our civilization is to barbarism. It is also true that we are increasingly extending the meaning of the sanctity of life by stressing the duty of the community to be compassionate towards those individuals who cannot care properly for themselves. Every affluent country continuously raises the standards by which it judges need. We are not prepared just to defend life but we insist upon looking at the quality of that life and upon trying to see how best to improve it. In these circumstances we are also working to see that the right to life should mean as much to every man—whether he be black or white, Asian or European. This is surely an essential part of the road we are trying to travel. It would, therefore, be both a disaster and a cruel paradox if, at the very time we had learned that to protect life was not enough, we began to fail even to uphold the minimum right.

We often criticize former centuries when the theory of behaviour was not matched by the practice. We see periods when the sanctity of human life was trumpeted abroad but when slavery and child prostitution were accepted. We even look back to more recent times when life was protected but there was no real attempt to give to the life of the huge mass of the population any of the qualities which respect for the personality and freedom from poverty and disease, demand. Today all Western nations are seeking to make good that position and it is against this which the concepts of permissiveness stand.

The right to make an individual judgment on a matter of

morals is fine until we place it in the context in which all such decisions have to be made. We are not only individuals, we live in a community and the responsibilities of the community towards the individual within it are everywhere increasing. Just as the State feels that it must limit freedom in the economic sphere so it sees that it must protect its citizens by the creation of a system of social welfare. In each of these ways the interrelation between the citizen and the community becomes more important. It is therefore essential that as he asks more of the community he must expect to contribute more. That contribution may merely be in terms of taxes or information, but it can be demanded in more personal terms. It may be that we are asked by the community to bear the special burden of a deformed child or his incurable mother in order that the lives of others may be safeguarded. In any case it does not seem unreasonable that, for the great end of the protection of human life, the community should insist that individuals should bear the burdens imposed by its refusal to sanction mercy-killing or abortion.

Are there then other responsibilities which the community can similarly demand? Until recently the answer would certainly have been yes, and a whole list of restrictions of personal activity, and particularly sexual activity, would be presented. There were things which were actually illegal like homosexual behaviour, incest, and bestiality and others which the State frowned on like adultery and fornication. It was up to good citizens not to offend against these mores or the fabric of society would be torn apart. In a very real sense people did not see such actions as purely private matters but thought instead that they harmed society as a whole. It is then to this whole area of sexual morality that we must now address ourselves. It is here that the Sunday newspapers in Europe and the *National Inquirer* and its fellows in the U.S.A. find most of the material they need for their castigation of the permissive society. There is no doubt that the sexual issues are, with drugs, those which most trouble the opponents of the permissive society and which give rise to a very high proportion of the very real problems encountered by its supporters.

4 Sexual Activity

Sex is fun. That would seem to be the proper note on which to start this chapter. I rather suspect that many commentators on the subject are so busy getting on to what St Paul thought about it or how Brigid Brophy thinks it is the most natural means of communication, that they do not linger long enough over the central proposition. Yet this is the claim for sex which is being made in the advertisements, in the newspapers, and on television every day. As the couple strolls beside a fast-running stream, arm in arm, her head on his shoulder, they smoke their menthol cigarettes and the world is good. Sex is enjoyable. To read the solemn proponents of the New Morality you'd have thought it was much more a matter of agonizing decision-making while the political radicals get so breathless about integrity that you begin to wonder whether it isn't less a matter of personal pleasure and more a service to the Party. I like George Orwell's insistence that the relationship between Winston and Julia was not just the expression of freedom in a world of regimentation but that they enjoyed themselves. 'Winston said "You like doing this? I don't mean simply me. I mean the thing in itself?" "I adore it," replies Julia.'

Now it does seem important to start a specific discussion of the permissive society and sex with the assertion that, whatever else may be true, at its centre there is a pleasurable act. This is not just because we need to be prevented from getting too solemn about it, but also because it is precisely this element that is continually thrust upon the public through the mass media. This was perhaps the secret of the success of the film *Tom Jones*, a merry romp in which the amatory adventures of the hero are unattended by any responsibilities, psychological traumas, unwanted babies, or moral earnestness. This is the message of those advertising pictures of two young lovers, kissing at the water's edge in the cool of the evening. Diamonds being forever are quite incidental, the fantasy is the eternal one of pleasure, unattended by responsibility or complication.

Thus when it is said that advertisements sell through sex it is not true. Advertisements sell their products by appealing to that ideal *fantasy* of sex which we all have—the sort of Garden-of-Eden picture with no tree of knowledge, no serpent, and no problems. This is, of course, romantic but then most of us are in fact romantics when it comes to sex—as the romantic novelists, the women's magazines, and the advertising industry are perfectly well aware. The fact that sex is fun is just one aspect, the fantasy is that it is fun and nothing more. We all cherish Gauguin-like dreams of South-Sea paradises with happy people running around in the sun in grass skirts enjoying themselves. It's all rather spoilt by the deserted wife and children at home, the disease and the death and as it's spoilt we prefer not to think about the drawbacks. It is a measure of John Cleland's art that in reading *Fanny Hill* we are able willingly to suspend our disbelief and indulge precisely this fantasy without the chill wind of realism ever blowing. It is the danger of his art and of our fantasy that it should prove so attractive that we believe that life should be like that and that in some way we can make it like that, if only we throw off our inhibitions and society's censure. The feeling is much like that old advertisement for the nudist movement—'Take off your clothes and live'. Somehow or other, if only we can break out of the constraints and conventions of clothes we shall be free of the complications of life by which we are affronted.

And we do feel affronted that sex is not simple, particularly in adolescent years when we first face the problems. Some get over it by ignoring all difficulties and adopting the 'Tom Jones' approach, others become so daunted by the complications that they take refuge in that technical chastity which is begotten of lack of opportunity out of fear and repression. A few try to face up to the problem—and most of us vacillate between all three attitudes.

Problem it certainly is. It is not just that sex is more than just fun; it is also that we continue to feel cheated because it has complications and our fantasy cannot become a reality. This is why Kenneth Tynan is so determined to make us believe that pornography is healthy entertainment—he desperately wants to find a way in which sex can be fun and nothing more.

Now it used to be reasonably easy to put up a case to young people which showed that, whatever one may wish, in actual cold light of dawn, sex also often involved having babies. There were a number of other attendant problems, such as the fact that men operated the double standard of expecting to have a permissive youth themselves while still preferring their wives to be virgins. The coming of the Pill has changed all this. We now seem to be within an ace of realizing the fantasy. The fact that in practice we have not sorted things out only points to the shallowness of the arguments of an older generation aiming to convince its children of the importance of chastity. It's not just that you might have a baby. It is that the human spirit demands more than the superficial and at the same time that it is asking for something deeper, it is wishing that it could be satisfied with the simple. We realize that sex is the means of consummating the deepest of personal relationships and at the same time we want it to be just a roll in the hay.

It would be easier were this really just a spirit versus flesh battle but it is precisely because there are elements of both in each understanding that it is so difficult. We want the simple view of sex not just because it is physically fun but because it *does* express beauty and joy. We demand the deeper and more satisfying relationship not just for spiritual reasons but because the physical pleasure is more rewarding. There is an immensely attractive spontaneity about the one and a vital totality about the other. Of course it is impossible to divide the two situations as absolutely as I have suggested but it is vital that we should accept the fact of the attractions of the promiscuous as well as those of the deepest kind of love. This is important not just because it is true, but because moralists of all kinds talk as if the argument can be restricted to a dialogue between those who think sex outside marriage is all right as long as you really are in love and those who think you have got to be married. That is not the argument at all. The real argument is whether free love is acceptable or whether there is any moral reason which would lead us to restrict sexual intercourse within the stable relationship of marriage. The first is a legalistic argument, the second is a real clash of opposing attitudes.

This is the reason that the New Morality men seem so old-fashioned when one reads their books published only in the mid-1960s. For Canon Douglas Rhymes, for example, the problems seem to be centred around the difficulties of the young couple who are deeply in love but must wait to get married. In fact, the real question is whether we have anything convincing to say to people about pre-marital sex in a society where birth control is widespread, young people are subject to minimal controls, and the mass media do everything possible to confirm our fantasies that sex should just be fun. It is a question we rarely face.

The Victorians were, of course, right about birth control. Its coming *has* made the question of sexual morality much more difficult. They felt that it would lead to loose behaviour and they condemned it on that ground. It was indeed only the patient work of people like Marie Stopes, who saw in birth control the emancipation of the mother from the annual pregnancy, that finally broke down the opposition which had sought to stop the spread of knowledge because it believed that it would spread immorality.

What in fact it has done is to open up a whole new debate about sex which previously did not arise merely because it was clearly irresponsible to risk bringing a child into the world outside the security of marriage. There really was little moral argument about it. You could have the 'sowing the wild oats' kind of excuse but you could hardly suggest that such a relationship was 'sacramental'! At the same time as such a discussion becomes practically possible, so the advent of psychology gives it a language. Not only can we choose more freely how we are to use our sexual instincts but we can see more clearly what those instincts amount to. It is the debate which these two factors have made possible which has forced the legislators of every Western country to look at how moral behaviour is regulated and how far the assumptions on which such regulation has been based can be justified in the new, post-Freudian conditions.

No country in the West has attempted to regulate the private behaviour of its population as far as fornication or adultery is concerned. At least, in those few states where there are laws on the statute book they have not been used in this century. At the same time, every country has laws to protect minors and to regulate prostitution, homosexuality and incest. Very few societies actually prohibit prostitution, they merely treat the symptoms by banning soliciting, making it illegal to live on immoral earnings, and ensuring that the normal legal protection afforded to citizens in their dealings with each other do not apply to known prostitutes. Thus we always have in practice been permissive about fornication and adultery and even about prostitution. That is not to say that the State has held no views on these activities. The moral earnestness which marked Christian and secularist alike in the nineteenth century has continued almost to the present in that it has been assumed by legislators that such behaviour is to be deplored even though experience has shown that it cannot be affected by legal sanctions. Indeed in some cases the *possibility* of extra-marital sexual activity is denied as was shown in one recent case tried in a British court. The plaintiff was suing his firm for damages for an industrial injury. His counsel claimed that the man, a batchelor of twenty-eight had found that the accident had considerably interfered with his sex life. At this, the judge remarked that, since the man was unmarried, he really could not see what sex life he could have! Such a comment has always been pretty wide of the mark but is obviously totally without reality in a society in which our attitudes have changed because of the advance in birth control techniques.

We live in a community in which pre-marital sexual intercourse is an accepted feature of life. It always has been fairly generally accepted, at least as far as males were concerned, as the parish registers of Europe with their records of hurried marriages and bastard children will confirm. Indeed one English rector in the eighteenth century got so tired of entering children as 'base born' that he shortened it to the initials B.B. Still the very high risk of pregnancy did mean that until very recently such behaviour could be stigmatized, even in the most worldly sense, as irresponsible. Today, apart from those with strong and traditional religious convictions or a real understanding and demand for the deepest of relationships, Western societies must proceed on the assumption that the majority of young people will sleep together outside the marriage bond.

It is odd that we have been so unwilling to face up to the consequences of this fact. We acknowledge it, perhaps bemoan it, but we make no real provision for it, either educationally or publicly. Only in Scandinavia is there any concerted attempt to teach children the techniques of birth control and the dangers of venereal disease. In the rest of Europe and in most of the U.S.A., society is managing to have the very worst of both worlds. By its advertisements and its pop heroes, by its very life-style, it is busy lauding the delights of romance to each new generation and yet it refuses to equip the majority of them, who will accept the values which are thrown at them daily, with the means to protect themselves and society from the more direct consequences of permissiveness.

This really is the sort of double standard which must destroy society. Either we decide that we intend to build a community in which traditional mores shall be promoted wholeheartedly or we accept the consequences of a society in which times really have changed. As the first proposition is a non-starter in any free society, then we must stop salving our consciences by omitting from school curricula relevant sex instruction. This may be impossible in France and Italy until there are changes in the State's attitude to birth control but it really does make sense in both Britain and the U.S.A.

In both countries there is a perfectly understandable reaction by parents who are bewildered by the changes in public mores and who dread what their children are going to make of them. They therefore tend to hold on to the one thing which seems to give them any hope—the possibility of keeping their children in ignorance. This attitude fits in neatly with the other wide-spread feeling that the subject of sex instruction is one which ideally ought to be left to the parents who are then able to explain it within the context of the personal values of the home. Together these attitudes have created formidable opposition to proper sex instruction in schools. In parts of America the amount of such instruction is actually declining as parents force school boards to discontinue sex lessons. In Britain it has meant that progress has been much slower than it could have been.

The risks that young people run are enormous. In the U.S.A. illegitimate births have increased by 350 per cent since 1940, cases of gonorrhoea by 76 per cent in ten years and syphilis increased alarmingly yet again in 1970. So dangerous is this that Dr James McKenzie—venereal disease Director of the American Social Health Association, called for 'national emergency action'

E

to curb the syphilis increase. In Denmark V.D. cases have risen by 40 per cent in one year—a statistic not widely quoted by the pro-pornography lobby—and in Britain there has been so startling an increase that the word 'epidemic' is now widely used.

Nevertheless, before we dismiss all such opposition to sex instruction as guilt-ridden traditionalism, it is as well to look at the very real fears which people have of some of those bodies campaigning for sex instruction in schools. There is a world of difference between intelligent teaching of the facts about contraception and venereal disease as part of a balanced programme which emphasizes the real value of human personality and the lasting union of man and wife, and the superficial cant which is put out by individuals like Martin Cole or organizations like the National Secular Society. So often the material which is produced seems entirely designed to divorce sex from any kind of moral teaching. The purpose of these people seems not to be concerned with the real human values involved and they certainly want to see that no religious values come into consideration. Their approach to sex teaching is indeed a prescription for compulsory permissiveness. It is not the reasoned reaction of a society which, although conscious of the continuing value of the high standards which real human relations demand, is prepared to face the fact of widespread permissiveness and provide against its direct effects. It is instead the attempt to create a society in which children are taught that totally permissive behaviour is the sensible way; that lifelong marriage is in no sense an ideal; and that there is no such thing as perversion as long as you enjoy it.

In case it might be thought that this is to put the position too strongly it is important to quote the advice given to young people by novelist and television personality, Miss Brigid Brophy in her introduction to a pamphlet entitled *Sex Education* written by Maurice Hill and Michael Lloyd-Jones for the National Secular Society. She first establishes that there should be no attempt to teach sex within a moral context. Quoting a letter to the *Guardian* newspaper as 'appeasing the obscurantists' by stating that 'sex education in primary schools has been designed to counter promiscuity', she lets us know that this would be 'propaganda for irrationality . . .' The information is needed not only by the temperamentally promiscuous but by those 'whose temperament will lead them to live with one person all their lives.' Having neatly disposed of any discussion as to whether fidelity is better than promiscuity either for the individual or society, she gallops on to deal with deviation. 'Sex education should stop endorsing society's irrational prejudice against homosexuality.' This is evidently because 'if education is in the least concerned with culture, it has no business to imply to its pupils that they are in a position to feel condescending pity towards Proust, Michelangelo, Socrates, Tchaikovsky, Sappho, E. M. Forster and Ronald Firbank.' She fails to include in her list; Nero, the Nazi Röhm, Gilles de Rais and William Rufus, whose nastiness had as little to do with their homosexuality as her hero-figures' excellence had to do with theirs.

After the helpful historical thoughts Miss Brophy turns to provide some direct advice to girls on how to handle their sex problems. 'You have the advantage of being able to masturbate rather more secretly than boys can, because your physiology leaves no traces. Your masturbating is no one's business but your own, so privacy is appropriate. Make the most of it. You might find it useful to practise coming quickly, in case you take as your lover a boy who hasn't been fortunate enough to read Maurice Hill and Michael Lloyd-Jones. If your lovers are to be girls, the need to hurry is one minor nuisance, among several others, which you will luckily avoid. If you turn out bisexual you will want to practise both speediness and prolongation, which should make for admirably varied masturbatory experience. I, too, hope you enjoy it—and also that it will bring enough relaxation and peace of mind for you to turn your energies to bullying our education system into providing you with a decent training for your mind. You urgently need to be able to think independently and to earn your living. Only then will you be free. You will be free to take several lovers of either sex, if that's how your temperament sways you. You won't be forced to make your lovers suspect you're trying to trick them into marrying and supporting you, and you won't be a poor dearie whom they stay with only out of pity. You will also be able to opt for celibacy, if you prefer it (you may find your own sexual company more entertaining than other people's). Celibacy is a luxury uneducated women cannot afford. Even if your temperament leads you to a lifetime union with one man, you will find that only when you are financially independent are you free to love him. Only if you could afford to leave him can you be quite sure that you are staying with him because you love him and not because he's your meal ticket.'

Now there's a fine preparation for any girl setting out on life! No wonder parents are not entirely happy about the prospect of some kinds of sex instruction in schools. Miss Brophy does at least dispose of the popular supposition that it is possible to teach sex instruction without any moral context. Her version is full of moral judgements—almost all of which are clearly opposed both to the wishes and the interests of society.

Western civilization is based on a community where the family is the most important unit. The stability and permanence of that unit is clearly shown by modern psychological investigation to be an even more important factor in the development of children than we suspected. The examples of the damage done by family breakdown and strife, of the problems created in children of one-parent families, and of the links between anti-social behaviour and family disturbance are so numerous as to be overwhelming. Yet increasingly we see actual physical effects of parental strife on their children. In their paper in the *New England Journal of Medicine*, four doctors from the Johns Hopkins Hospital, Baltimore, showed that in their study of children who grew abnormally slowly they did so because of the 'emotionally disturbed environment' of their homes and that removal from that environment was the only way in which to restore their growth to its normal rate.

What a foolish myth it is that we can regulate our conduct without regard to its effect on others. Society is in a real sense the guardian of its children and its first duty must be to create the conditions most likely to foster a secure family relationship. Of course it is wrong to pretend that merely keeping parents together saves a marriage. Successful marriages have to be worked for and cannot be forcibly imposed through legal sanctions of indissolubility. Yet it will not help the building of real marriages if girls are told that the choice between promiscuity and fidelity is a mere matter of 'temperament'—whatever that may mean. If it is considered a matter of indifference how sex is used, as long as one's technique is right and one's enjoyment sufficient, then it is hardly likely that girls will see the need to build the stable relationship so necessary if children are to be properly brought up. There really can be very few who think, with Miss Brophy, that it is a matter of indifference whether one's sexual behaviour is homosexual, heterosexual, or bi-sexual, or that the idea of lifelong union is one choice among a whole range of differing possibilities. There must be even fewer who can equate celibacy with 'finding your own sexual company more entertaining than other people's'—even if they can fathom out any sensible meaning of the phrase. We must of course feel very sorry for Brigid Brophy. What a deprived and sad person she seems from this. Sex becomes only a sort of mechanical joy-ride dependent upon the temperament of the participant(s). Most people must feel she should have nothing to do with education in any community which has any concern about its children. When we demand sex instruction in our schools it is within a context in which the community can not only teach the facts of conception and contraception, but can also show to children the moral responsibilities involved as well as holding before them the example of the kind of family life which alone can produce balanced and healthy children. Sadly this is not Miss Brophy's idea of life nor indeed of proper instruction. It is therefore not surprising that some of the opposition to teaching of sex in schools comes from well-informed parents who would prefer their children to be taught the truth at home rather than imbibe progressive claptrap in the classroom.

It is, unfortunately, not enough to leave the teaching to the parents, although schools could do a lot more through the parent-teacher associations in encouraging parents to explain to their children about sex and perhaps help them with the right books and information. There is still a primary responsibility upon the schools as the community's educational medium to see to it that a generation which grows up among so much which invites sexual experiment, should understand about contraception and the prevention of disease and at the same time be shown that there are important concerns of moral responsibility and value in personal relationships which may lead many individuals to oppose the prevailing permissive view.

This is most important if the permissive society is not to become a compulsive society as far as sex is concerned. All of us are to some extent creatures of fashion and the younger we are the more likely we are to be swayed by the popular view and accepted attitude of our peer groups. It is now almost impossible for young people living in the average urban situation of Europe and America to uphold anything other than permissive standards. We have moved from a society in which it was made extremely difficult for people to be other than chaste, to one in which all the pressures are towards promiscuity. The market researchers tell the young that everybody does it and the popular magazines say that those few who don't, have said 'no to life' or, more likely, are abnormal. Every method of communication and every kind of advertising make sex at one and the same time the all-important thing in life and a most trivial experience suitable for selling deodorant soap. There is indeed a great need for self-discipline in the mass media if we are not to exchange compulsory abstinence for compulsory free love. There is also a great need for the kind of teaching in our schools which would do something to support parents in offering an alternative view of the rôle of sex in real life.

If then we are to continue to look towards the stable family unit as necessary for society, what ought we to think about the movement towards easier divorce? There is no doubt that this has gathered considerable strength in recent years. Italy has now introduced divorce for the first time; in Britain there is now divorce without consent after desertion; and in the U.S.A. even those states which upheld traditional codes are removing the tougher provisions of their laws. There ought to be no disagreement with the contention that it does not create a stable marriage to keep two people living together just because there is no means by which they can split up. It ought also to be agreed that it would be a mistake so to ease the divorce arrangements that marriage became an impermanent institution in the mind of a community. As the evidence for the need for childhood stability mounts, so the determination of the community to protect the permanent nature of the family should increase.

These two contentions should lead us to acknowledge both the need for divorce in a secular State, whatever our religious view on the matter may be, and also to accept the fact that the State must have an important say in the way in which marriage and divorce is conducted. The concept of divorce by consent is basically unacceptable because it suggests that the community has no interest in the arrangement which has been made. This becomes an increasingly less tenable position as the community assumes greater obligations towards individuals and therefore has a greater right to demand responsibility in return. If we accept the stable marriage as an aim worthy of the State's concern then we ought to move closer to the concept of breakdown of marriage as the ground for divorce rather than demanding some sort of marital offence. This was certainly the view of the Church of England's admirable investigation into the issue, *Putting Asunder,* and it has largely influenced the new divorce law which came into force in Britain in 1971. The very nature of this new law is to support the view that society has a vested interest in the creation and retention of stable marriages. The emphasis which it places on attempts at reconciliation before an irretrievable breakdown is considered to have taken place, exactly underlines the duty of the community to do all it can to protect the family.

Nevertheless, it leaves unanswered the problem which was highlighted in Britain by Baroness Summerskill, namely that economically Western society is organized so that men can afford only one family and that our rising expectations are such that this will continue to be the case. The problem of getting maintenance out of men who have set up home afresh is a common one in any court and the real hardship of women left to fend for themselves after twenty years of marriage cannot be brushed away in the easy terms which some libertarians employ.

Yet breakdown in marriage is bound to occur increasingly in a society which is not prepared to accord to the family the importance which it really possesses. One of the saddest things about the American scene is that the inability of the older generation to communicate the value of the central relationship in a family has led to a new generation for whom it has less and less meaning. Their upbringing in which the stability and authority of the family was often so ineffective leads them to believe that it is all a myth—that such a family cannot exist— that a happy marriage is an idyllic sham which hardly anyone

attains and which is not worth striving for. It is in combating
this cynical view that public pressure for the assertion of community values is so essential. In the consideration of drugs and
delinquency, pornography and violence which follows, the
community's rôle must continually be kept in mind.

There is nothing wrong in demanding that the community
should hold views about these matters. After all, it is inevitable.
If the community allows Miss Brophy's arid attitude to have
currency in its schools then it is taking a stand that promiscuity
and fidelity are equally unimportant as far as society is concerned. If it demands that children should be taught the value
of the family and learn something of the need for fidelity, the
practice of marital communication, and the place of sex in
that relationship then it is merely taking a different stand. The
real contrast is not between objective science and moral brain-
washing, which is what the secularists would have us believe.
It is between community support for its own destruction and
community concern for the next generation.

It is that same concern for the next generation which must
give the community the right to discourage deviant behaviour.
It is obviously nonsense to go on locking people up for abnormal
sexual activities between consenting adults. This is still the
pattern in France, and some other European countries, and
certain states in the U.S.A. Yet to agree that it is neither effective nor sensible to punish homosexuals is not to support the
growing tendency which would demand that society should in
no way pass judgement on such behaviour. This is to ignore the
facts of history which show that the attitude of society in general
can have a major effect upon the amount of homosexual and
other deviant activity. The Greeks of classical times were not
biologically or psychologically different from ourselves but the
society which they created actively encouraged homosexual
behaviour and it is therefore not very surprising that it was
much more widespread than it has been in other civilizations.
If we believe as a community that it is a mark of our civilization
that we are beginning to stop persecuting people whose sexual
development has been abnormal we ought also to be able to
say that we wish to protect as many people as possible from the
difficulties which deviation involves. We shall not say with
Desmond Morris that society will confer on homosexuals

special favour because they help to lessen population pressures but we will continue to try to create a society in which the encouragement is towards normal development.

It is this environmental duty of society which will concern us particularly. So often we think of the State's choice as if it were between compulsion and permission. Very often it is much more complicated. The community must decide the sort of society which is most likely to encourage the development of its people and its own continuance. To do this it may well have to discourage activities which it cannot or will not make unlawful. It will certainly have to take a stand on certain moral issues even though it has no intention of forcing people to obey its moral dictates. In education it is impossible for the State to be neutral and therefore it has to make a choice of the values which it wishes to place before its children. In facing up to its responsibilities towards those who cannot carry them themselves it has to decide what its duty is in protecting the unborn child, the terminally ill, and the chronically depressed. Above all it cannot stand aside and believe that its environmental responsibilities stop with river pollution and mercury in tuna fish. It has to accept that its decisions or lack of decisions on moral issues are going to have the most direct bearing upon the environment in which each new generation grows up and that fundamentally concerns the community.

5 Literature and the Permissive Society

If the coming of the permissive society has occasioned a major change in our actual behaviour and the laws which govern it then it has been even more noticeable in its effect upon the way we write about that behaviour. Some material which we now take for granted in television plays would never have been broadcast even as recently as five years ago. Despite the current reaction against violence on American television there is no doubt that in general all Western nations are much freer in what they see as acceptable for general dissemination. The frontiers have been pushed back and, as is so often the case, the effect has been to concentrate attention upon each small step in the movement and justify that, rather than consider the question as a whole.

Before the invention of the printing press there was very little need for the censorship of pornography. The Romans had a stab at it, particularly under the Christian emperors, but throughout the Middle Ages censorship was really concerned with matters of heresy as books were largely religious in nature, and writing and copying was centred on the religious communities where heresy would of course be a matter of great moment. Such popular writing as there was very often contained bawdy jokes and dirty stories upon which there was very little attack.

After the Reformation censorship on grounds of pornography is often extremely difficult to disentangle from censorship for political or religious reasons. Most countries operated some sort of licensing system which further complicates any attempt at isolating specific cases of objection to pornography. During the second half of the seventeenth century and the eighteenth century European manners were sufficiently broad to allow both the Restoration playwrights and the earliest novelists free rein. *Fanny Hill* was thought a little extreme and Cleland was given a pension in order to stop him writing further such volumes. Otherwise pornography circulated with little hindrance and it was not until the nineteenth century that the growth of popular reading led governments to take any firm steps to restrict the sale of pornographic literature. It is, therefore, essential to see that censorship of pornographic material has always been bound up with a consideration of who is going to read it. It was the coming of the mass market and the opportunity to exploit that market which pushed the Victorians into the 'business' of censorship.

The nineteenth century was prolific in its production of pornography. There were the usual novels of amatory adventures and a number of magazines with serials of various kinds catering for people of differing tastes. There was a good deal of sadism, the birch providing endless tales, and a staple diet of stories of the initiation of young people into the delights of sex, with particular emphasis on the seduction of young footmen by their mistresses. This was, however, largely a metropolitan business and circulation was among the wealthier classes. The trade was attacked widely and in 1857 Lord Campbell's Act sought to suppress it. Success was marginal and much less important than the effect of public taste upon literary production. Underworld publishing was kept in check by the pornography laws but by no means eradicated. The real censor was articulate opinion which kept literature clean through the censorship imposed by the circulating libraries and through the activities of the reviewers who were quick to spot any crudity of phrase or plot.

In 1853 the Customs were specifically empowered to seize any pornographic material which came in from abroad and in 1870 the Post Office Act made it an offence to send indecent material through the public mail.

Up to the last years of the nineteenth century there were few serious authors either in Europe or America for whom the effect of the law or public opinion was onerous. The law and the censorship of the lending libraries were hardly challenged as there was no one whose subject matter was essentially of a kind to infuriate either in Britain. It was the Bradlaugh case, when a book on birth control was declared obscene by two lower Courts and only saved on a technicality in the High Court, that saw the beginning of the change. There followed a series of cases as authors began to step outside the boundaries established by the combined power of the law and public taste. In this the British example furnishes a copybook case and is worth following through as it is uncomplicated by Supreme Court rulings and State's rights as is the American story. There was the trial of Havelock Ellis's *Sexual Inversion*, the cases against *Ulysses*, *The Well of Loneliness*, *The Naked and the Dead*, and *The Philanderer*. As a result of this last case there was a growing demand among publishers and authors for the law to be changed and above all clarified. It was haphazardly enforced at what appeared to be the whim of the police and the particular Home Secretary. For example, Mr Justice Stable's liberal views in summing up the case on *The Philanderer* had not stopped Sir Gerald Dodson giving what appeared to be precisely opposite instructions to the jury in the case of *September in Quinze*. The result of this pressure was the introduction and passing of the Obscene Publications Act (1959).

In concept this Act was intended to allow publication of any work which, taken as a whole, had a serious literary purpose and was intended to be treated as a normal publication. This would leave the law mainly to deal with material which was manifestly pornographic and whose purpose was to excite sexually. This had usually been the aim of moderate reformers; they wanted to make sure that works of literature were allowed while avowedly pornographic material was restricted. It is a relatively new departure that people should openly campaign for the legalization of pornography and it has been a departure which has pushed moderate reformers, like Sir Alan Herbert, out of the anti-censorship lobby into the company of those who would retain some restrictions.

His position, however, is attacked by most of the anti-censorship leaders. The pressure in all Western countries is in fact to get rid of all remaining censorship even of the avowedly pornographic. The position is a simple one and it can only reasonably be supported or rejected if we face up to the kind of material which such a liberalization of the law would allow. Up to the present this is material which has been condemned by all sides in the controversy and about which there has been no real argument.

The reasons for discounting the avowedly pornographic have, of course, differed from generation to generation. For the puritan it was to be viewed with moral superiority. The decent would soon find pornography sickening and only degraded persons could write or read it. Today the superiority remains but it has ceased to be moral and become psychological. The modern theory is that all normal people will find pornography boring after a certain initial amusement. Only the psychologically immature or incompetent will continue to read it and, far from doing harm, it releases their repressions and provides an outlet for their fantasies much less dangerous than those which they might otherwise seek. The puritan would conclude that pornography ought to be banned in order to protect the innocent. The modern view would be that pornography ought to be allowed or even encouraged for therapeutic reasons. There has it is true been no widespread demand as yet to make it available on the National Health or under Medicare but in Sweden pornographic literature is being provided in prison libraries to provide an outlet for the sexual frustrations of the prisoner and at least one psychiatrist in England has pleaded its value in helping long-term hospital patients.

Whatever the outcome of this sort of demand, there is no doubt that the campaign for the total abolition of literary censorship is gathering new strength throughout Western Europe and America. Increasingly there is a view which suggests that pornography only disgusts normal people because it is *bad* pornography and that were it allowed freely then the standards would rise after being artificially held down because such productions were illegal. Perhaps Kenneth Tynan is the most obvious spokesman for this attitude. He speaks with no superiority—either psychological or moral—he merely states that pornography can be diverting and that people who want to be so diverted should be allowed to be so. His is the basic cry for complete freedom which is perhaps most attuned to the attitudes of the permissive society. Just as he has lauded the pleasures of masturbation to the readers of the *Observer*, so he is a publicist for the pleasures of pornography in both England and America.

Yet whether the reason is because people will soon tire of pornography or because people will soon learn to like it, the Lilac Establishment is out to do for Britain and America what has been done in Denmark. There, following a much publicized prosecution of *Fanny Hill*, the right-wing Christian Minister of Justice, past middle age and representing a very traditionally minded constituency announced the abolition of all forms of censorship of pornography. His theory was simple: abolish censorship and you have no problem of where you should draw the line. Allow obscene literature and people will soon tire of it, the illicit attraction having been removed.

International agreements meant that a year had to elapse between the announcement of the change and its enactment. That year was perforce without police prosecution so that the pornography industry flourished. Shops selling 'Weekend Sex' and other creations of Leo Madsen spread throughout Copenhagen although the centre of the trade remained in the traditional red-light area of the city. Shops showed their wares in their windows leaving nothing to the imagination of passers-by. Business boomed and no year since has quite measured up to that first one when pornography was technically illegal but there were no prosecutions.

When the law was actually changed, the regulations insisted upon material being available only on request, genitals being decently covered in the windows; and children being unable to buy the goods. Where a shop obviously specializes in the sale of this kind of product—and it is quite easy to spot by the large sign 'Porno-Shop' or merely SEX—then books and magazines may be displayed on racks. Otherwise in your local news-agent's, for whom it is only a sideline, you actually have to ask for sex books and will then be handed a boxful. Should you be too shy to go into the shop or if its too early in the morning (it is difficult to be too late at night) then you can put your money into a slot-machine where the books are decently covered with strategic sticky paper, or more recently, with brown paper outer wrappers.

In effect, children can buy what they like. The police admit that they have no chance of stopping people selling to who ever asks and even if they did then slot machines cannot discrimin-ate. About half the clientèle of the shops consists of young men between fifteen and thirty. There can, of course, be no accurate figures but this impression, gained by random surveys seems widely accepted. The traditional liberal view that only old men with failing powers and ugly wives would patronize these establishments does seem to be contradicted by the facts. Indeed John Calder has faced up to this but excuses it rather flippantly when answering Pamela Hansford Johnson's comments on the success of the Danish Pornographic Fair. He finds it not at all 'surprising that many young Danes attracted by the publicity spend an hour or so going to an erotic exhibition, just as they would here'.

It is a good thing we are now all agreed that young people are attracted to pornographic exhibitions, whether by the publicity or not. It is interesting too that they are attracted even in a society where there are few inhibitions about extra-marital sexual intercourse. For many of these young men pornography is not acting as a release for the repressions but, *pace* Tynan, it is of interest in itself.

The other myth that ought to be exploded is the theory that in fact it is only tourists who buy these books and magazines and that if they were freely available throughout the world then the market would soon dry up. Apart from the obvious fact that there will always be a new generation of readers for whom the same attraction of novelty must continue, there is direct evidence to the contrary. In almost every shop in Denmark the majority of books which have text rather than illustrations are written in Scandinavian languages—principally Danish and Swedish. As neither language is widely spoken outside the mother country it is safe to assume that these books are intended for home consumption.

Yet what is really on sale? As Denmark can serve as a test case of what might happen in Britain and is happening in America, we ought to be perfectly clear what such freedom involves. Many of those who are vaguely on the side of lifting all censorship seem to think that it would simply mean the public sale of a few explicitly dirty books which would describe, with suitable variations of scene, heterosexual acts between two adults. There are, in fact, very few such books. Most of the non-illustrated pornography that is available has the added spice of multiple participants. Lesbian scenes seem obligatory as does a good deal of sadism. Many play on racialist sexual fantasies and tell of the adventures of convent-educated young ladies, holidaying in the Bahamas, whose attraction to the black waiters lead to their downfall—again and again. There is usually a section of male homosexual stories, usually orgiastic and containing detailed seductions of young boys. All this type of non-illustrated material is poorly printed on cheap paper but with fairly smart typographical covers. The books usually cost about 50p and are widely sold, not just in 'porno' shops but at railway stations, bus terminals and in ordinary bookshops. In fact this is in large measure the Danish version of the sort of book published by Midwood, Olympia, Regent House, or, rather less explicitly, by Bee Line in the U.S.A.

The real change that has been wrought in Sweden and Denmark is the explicitly sexual picture-story. The lifting of censorship has created a steady market for these booklets which no longer need to masquerade as art poses or examples of photographic technique. They are the first new product of freedom. The high quality colour printing and photography was only possible when this larger market was opened up. No under-the-counter operation could afford to produce material so well. Their success has made it possible to print in full colour on art paper. They contain pictures of sexual acts from all angles in what is often grotesque clarity. Each book tells a story in pictures with no text. Again, straightforward one-man-one-woman stories give too little scope and two men one girl, or, more often, two girls and one man are the norm. As in the textual books, lesbian sequences are almost *de rigueur* and it is quite clear that as the months since abolition have passed the producers have been forced into creating ever more inventive situations. There is an important fantasy element with copulation taking place in historical costumes, sometimes complete with masks, or in track suits in gymnasia, in nurses' uniforms in hospitals, or with doctors in their surgeries. Priests and nuns are now particularly popular, having replaced the vogue for policemen being seduced by lady traffic offenders.

Love has, of course, no part to play and even passion, as the writer Susan Sontag remarks, is conspicuously absent, and this contrasts noticeably with the most professional Japanese material. Each story follows a predictable pattern; the actors meet each other, they become friendly over a drink, they undress and copulate. The men sit back and watch the girls perform together which gives the opportunity to show huge anatomical photographs of genitals. Then everybody joins in together, doing whatever seems appropriate, until one grand communal climax is achieved.

Such books are often by-products of pornographic films—using the same actions and story-lines and, like the films, their tendency is towards an increasing degree of perversion. The story is given variety by extraordinary garbs and athletic feats and by multiplying the number of people involved. Everyone does everything possible to everyone else and the photographs are intensely specific—particularly in their depiction of ejaculation. Some books dispense with the story and merely show a whole series of the most 'special' poses.

This is, of course, the straightest type of pornography, provided for those of normal tastes and habits! There are also the parallel productions, designed for the homosexual market and referred to as 'homophil' magazines. In these, hitch-hiking, sports sessions, or art studios provide the environment for stories which are similarly explicit and usually involve more than two people. Other magazines cater for those who like rubberwear, plastic raincoats or little girls. There is usually a good selection of books for the 'flag' market—those interested in flagellation and bondage. It seems to be difficult to make these realistic as volunteers for 'actors' and 'actresses' are limited. Nevertheless, where many are pathetic tableaux, some are realistically cruel.

There are laws to stop minors acting as models in these photographs but the manufacturers do seem to have discovered some remarkably slow developers as stand-ins. There is a whole series devoted to animal pornography—each featuring a girl with a different animal. In general the models used are attractive, but as after the first few snaps the photographs are largely confined to those of the genital regions, this is of little practical import.

Thus these illustrated books, priced at about £1, cover almost every imaginable taste—there are even those which are purely auto-erotic. There is also a sort of pornographic version of the popular magazine called *Week-end Sex*. This is a weekly publication with articles and captioned picture strips. The content is largely heterosexual although most of it involves more than two people but there is a regular homosexual picture feature and

F

occasionally other tastes are introduced. The suggestion is that
the magazine will help to add variety to one's married life and
that it therefore ought to be bought together with the week-end
shopping. Indeed the manufacturers are particularly keen on
suggesting that a great deal of this material is bought by ordinary married couples who are seeking to improve what would
otherwise be a rather run-of-the-mill married life.

In Denmark and Sweden the situation is indeed one of complete freedom with every taste provided for. There are two
hundred firms involved in the business of which twelve or so
are substantial. The daily newspapers carry advertisements for
private parties to suit every taste as well as for books and all
kinds of useful sexual gadgets. The 'porno' shops themselves
also sell series of photographs in packs, vibrators, massagers,
and home movie films. There is no attempt to make you buy
any of the material on sale and people often appear to be just
browsing. Occasionally the curious calm hush which these
shoppers share with early morning churchgoers is broken by
the entry of a bus load of German trippers but otherwise they
shuffle round and read until they have chosen a purchase and
had it wrapped in the distinctive brown bags which all the shops
seem to use.

The other two Scandinavian countries, Norway and Finland,
do not have such lax laws but of course a great deal of pornographic material is brought in over the border by returning
nationals. The books are largely produced in Denmark and
southern Sweden and the models are recruited locally—usually
among students looking for a way to make extra money. Some
of the girls do seem to feel doubtful about it but have agreed
because of the money or because their friends are also involved.
The men tend to present it as a harmless lark which has the
advantage of paying well although rather less well than for the
girls. Neither sex is usually willing to admit to posing for anything other than boy/girl photographs but in fact almost everyone
involved must be prepared at least to join in multiple sex acts.

There are two or three large operators in the field who
publish, edit and distribute the books. Besides the shops they
run large mail order businesses with a high proportion of customers in Great Britain and Germany. This is, strictly, illegal as
Denmark is a subscriber to the International Postal Union

which proscribes the mailing of pornographic material. In practice little is done by the Danish government to prevent abuses of this agreement and the trade is therefore a major earner of foreign exchange for a country which has a balance of payments problem.

Nowhere in the rest of the Western world is pornography so freely available. Wholesalers from other countries come to Denmark and pick up films and sex books which they then smuggle over the border. Material bound for the U.S.A. usually goes via Holland as the American customs are wary of packages from Denmark. To overcome the laws in Britain, at least four British producers operate out of Denmark.

In Germany there are sex supermarkets but they are much more limited in what they are able to offer publicly. Most English language non-illustrated pornography is on ready sale throughout the Federal Republic but its source is almost entirely American. Similarly, American hard-core pornography is on sale in countries like Italy and Greece which have strict laws governing the sale of such material in their own language. Curiously there is a much wider selection of books to suit every taste at Leonardo da Vinci airport in Rome than there is at Copenhagen and Stockholm airports. In Holland the sale of English-language pornography is widespread and a major feature of most railway bookstalls. Again its source is almost entirely American. In the red-light area of Amsterdam there are pornography shops but the State restricts what can be shown so that most of the illustrated material is of the naturist magazine type. Persistence will produce further products on Danish lines but this is not publicly on sale.

In Britain, most large towns have bookshops where pornographic literature may be bought but it is very much more restricted in type. In London the shops have mushroomed over the past five years although they are still largely concentrated in Soho. Most are controlled by one syndicate which provides the merchandise and owns some of the shops. The material on public show largely masquerades as naturist and sun-loving or is of the American glossy fantasy kind, with models dressed up in all manner of strange garbs. Full frontal nudity in both sexes has recently become possible but sexual acts may not be portrayed nor any signs of excitement.

Inside the shops things are very different from the Danish pattern. The books are in cellophane so that they cannot be handled and very soon the attendant will ask if you are looking for anything in particular. If you ask for something 'stronger', once he has ascertained that you are not the police, he will release the catch and allow you inside his inner room, where reposing in a large suitcase for easy transport are the real pornographic books at prices from £5 upwards.

In general this consists of duplicated novels complete with amateurish stencilled illustrations, various titles from Denmark, and packs of cards which are captioned and tell a story. These books are not in cellophane but are there for careful perusal before purchase. They are sold on a semi-hire basis and can be traded in at half-price when you return for a further title. According to the trade there does not seem to be any pattern of what sells best, although there are very few definite fashions and a particular taste will predominate for a few weeks and then another take its place. Altogether the practical situation in Britain is that all kinds of pornographic literature is available, but only to those who can afford it and who take some trouble to get it.

There has also been a growing tendency to sell pornographic material through the post. After the Danish Sex Fair, for example, many people received unsolicited cyclostyled letters from a Hamburg-based company Carl Vinter. The letters were particularly distressing as they suggested that the names and addresses had been obtained from someone who had previously sold such material to the addressee, who was therefore 'a thoroughly reliable person'. The effect of this in many perfectly respectable households must have been very upsetting. Mr Vinter claimed to be able to supply the best books, photos, and films—'bluer than blue, Lesbian, male/male; male/female; and group action in all the best sex positions'. Money was to be paid to his London agent who lived in Leytonstone. Prices ranged from photo books at £3 to reading books at £4— both with discounts for bulk orders.

All this contravenes the Post Office Act, the Customs regulations and probably the Exchange Control Act then obtaining. In any case there is certainly a good deal of this material coming into all countries with anti-pornographic laws. Control is difficult, but in Britain there have been a number of prosecutions and the Customs are continually seizing consignments of material. In 1968–9 1½ million books and magazines were seized. There has, of course, been particular complaint of a book on the various possible positions for sexual intercourse advertised by the Julian Press. Again the material has come unsolicited, sent out to mailing lists which do seem to include that of a well known credit card company. This was a warning printed in red at the top, followed by the message 'All the photographic illustrations of the variations of position possible in sexual intercourse contained in this book are posed by unclothed human models.' In this case the Post Office has connived at the advertisement, as a business reply envelope which they have licensed, is included.

Agitation against this kind of sale through the post has grown in the United States recently where many parents have begun to check their post before young children pick it up because over fifty million mailing pieces a year of an explicitly sexual kind are sent out to American homes and increasingly direct statements have been appearing on the outside of the envelopes. It often appears that as long as the book or film advertised inside can be called sex education material the U.S. Postal Service will take no action. Whether the recently passed laws enabling a citizen to register as someone who does not wish to receive pornographic material will have much effect is still too early to say. Under these provisions a register of such people is compiled and continually updated so that any firm sending out material of a sexual nature must buy the register and will be liable to a very heavy fine if it sends to any person recorded therein. There is certainly good reason in the U.S.A. to wish to restrict the enormous volume of pornographic material sent out by mail. As much of it masquerades as sex education literature, it is perhaps easier to understand the reaction of those parents in areas like California who have forced school boards to ban sex education in their schools.

The U.S.A. differs, of course, from state to state in its regulations concerning pornographic material. However, the situation in New York and California is much the same and comes somewhere between Britain and Denmark. *Life* magazine reckons that the business is worth £1 billion a year with very low overheads. Non-illustrated textbooks of the kind already mentioned as being widely distributed in Europe are, of course, available almost everywhere. The publishers even exhibit at the Frankfurt International Book Fair alongside ordinary book publishers and their books are distributed by major European distributors who carry perfectly respectable publishers as well. The great Random House business can hardly welcome the fact that one American publisher of 'adult' fiction calls itself Brandon House. As one would expect, there is some of the usual American euphemism when it comes to the presentation of these kind of books. There is indeed a continuing attempt to make them respectable—to give an excuse for people to buy— which is not found in Scandinavian non-illustrated erotica. Many titles will have an introduction by someone who is announced as a psychiatrist and who has M.D. after his name. He will write perhaps a page and a half of semi-scientific junk in order to suggest that the series of amatory adventures which follow shed new light on the problem of nymphomania, or homosexuality. In advertising too, these publishers like to suggest that there is something sociological, scientific, or even documentary about their books. For example, Regent House bind into their books a catalogue of their titles which they claim are 'Adult, Entertaining, Educational'. Each volume has its accompanying blurb. One is 'a timely insight into mail order sex' another 'a terrifying approach to capital punishment' a third is 'a dissection of an act of sexual violence and its effect upon the man who committed it.' Many of the titles are presented as if they were investigations into pressing moral problems and sometimes there are a few non-pornographic titles among the mass of sex books to raise the tone. Among more than three hundred books with titles like *The Sin Farm*, *The Endless Orgy*, *The Homo Farm*, and *The Shy Nymphomaniac* which appear in one catalogue comes, rather surprisingly, *You don't have to be bald*, *Nutrition, your key to good health*, and *Has Dr Max Gerson a true cancer cure?*

In the U.S.A. as in Scandinavia the racial fantasy is particu- larly well exploited and every cliché of the civil rights move- ment is twisted to this end. One book, *Integrated Intercourse*, is introduced thus:

'Is the mystery of black/white sex only skin deep? Since time immemorial white man has harboured in his fantasies the notion of a black man invested with supernatural [*sic*] sexual powers. And of the negro woman he has maintained the most guilt-ridden concept of all, venting towards her all the venom of his conflicted feelings, as one would towards an exotic captive beast whose mysterious allurements imprisoned him in his own fears. IS THIS THE HEIGHT OF DECADENCE, OR THE FLOWER- ING OF A NEW EPOCH IN MORALITY? The rage of change grips the country, and many see in its tide a decaying of values that may bring apocalypse in our time. The new black/white morality is a generic part of that wave, and thus not to be ignored, a genuine front on the numberless frontiers of research and learning. IS THIS A TRESPASS OF SOCIAL LIMITS OR A RETURN TO EDEN? Some see the world making a last sick fling before going down in flames and gnashing of teeth, while others firmly set forth the doctrines of a worldwide peace in whose advent the integrating of all races is a salient force. IS THIS A PERVERTED DESTRUCTION OF ALL MORES OR A STRIVING FOR UNITY THROUGH ALL MEN? Those who have doubts about interracial sex express the fear that chaos will reign if we do not have rules, while others believe that the sickness lives in the rule itself and it should be banished.'

You would hardly believe that all that pretentious rubbish is composed simply to sell a book of sex-positions involving two models—one of whom happens to be black. One has heard some pretty hair-raising claims for chastity but nothing to match this apologia for experiment!

As far as illustrated books are concerned, full frontal nudity has been accepted for some time although there were long battles as to whether a female model could be photographed with her legs apart and at what point arousal in the male could be said to have taken place. The first question has been answered affirmatively and the second geometrically. The pornographic shops in the U.S.A. do seem largely to be used by middle-aged and old men. These shops are clearly good business and have been expanding rapidly. Three years ago Manhattan had thirty 'porn' bookshops, now there are sixty and their profit margins are somewhere around 300 per cent. Young people tend to depend on newspapers sold at the kiosks, like the New York *Review of Sex*; *Sophisticated Swapper*; *Kiss*; *Screw*; and *Pleasure* (subtitled 'the newspaper you read with one hand'). These appear and disappear as the police clean them up or leave them alone. They are of varying quality both in terms of production and literacy. Their managements are intensely scornful of each other and *Screw* in particular taunts the others with being un-interested in the real matters of sexual freedom and concerned only with making money. It prides itself in fighting legal battles while, it says, the others just give in! They contain articles, photographs, and advertisements but much of the space is taken up by small ads. *Sophisticated Swapper* divides these into the various departments: 'female form', 'Male bag', 'french horn', 'Photo shop', 'the bizarre', 'group grab', 'gay blade' and 'dutch dyke'. All these contain details—some with accompanying photograph—stating the partner wanted and the interests expected. Respondents then send into the newspaper enclosing $1 and the reply is forwarded to the advertiser. The newspaper is thus able to charge for the original advertise-ment and for every reply it engenders. Ladies can advertise free, as can anyone including their photograph. These papers perform the same function as some serious newspapers in Denmark and at least here you do not need to buy them unless you want what you are getting. They advertise all sorts of sexual gear, detailed in the kind of trendy phraseology which makes it all sound compulsory for the up-to-date person, especially as excuses are carefully dropped into the text so that extremely ex-plicit photographs are introduced by phrases like, 'Marriage coun-sellors often recommend aids like these for connubial bliss.'

Much the same kind of operation is run in the United King-dom where there is no pretence at the magazines being any-thing other than printed Pandars. The advertisements range from offers of marriage to specific requests for specialist sexual interests. Clearly these magazines have a very wide readership. A very ordinary advertisement inserted by the editor of a famous British 'straight' magazine brought more than fifty replies; most of these were so frank that they had to be locked in the office safe while the article on the response to the advertisement was written, and then subsequently destroyed. To conform to the law these pamphlets all carry the following: 'It is an offence to send obscene or pornographic materials through the mail. Do not forget.'

In France, the pornography trade took a great knock when General de Gaulle tightened up the regulations at precisely the time at which other nations were loosening theirs. Paris had been the traditional home of the production of English-language pornography, as it had been the place where works of literature which had been banned in Great Britain and the U.S.A. were produced. The Olympia Press produced the first English versions of a number of books now considered classics and Maurice Girodias was at the centre of this publishing scene for many years. Recently a shop in Paris selling religious articles and church furnishings was found to be a major supplier of pornographic material in English and French and was closed by the police. Now most pornography is sold by the time-honoured expedient of approaching tourists in the street and offering 'special' picture postcards, although there are a few recognized places in the Pigalle area of Paris where the trade goes on.

Although the laws governing pornography vary widely in their rigour from country to country, there is not a nation in the Western world where pornography is not on sale in one way or another. In Spain and Portugal the traffic is small and centred around the tourists. In Denmark it is a major earner of foreign exchange and an important national industry. In all countries the student drug-culture newspapers usually contain a good deal of pornographic material, while in America it is a growing national and international business.

In the face of this general picture and having looked at precisely the kind of material with which we are concerned, we must look at the advisability of completely removing all forms of censorship of printed matter. The advocates for abolition say that you have pornography anyway so why not accept that and allow it so that people cannot make exorbitant profits out of the trade. If people are able to buy the material then they will soon get tired of it and the trade will collapse. This argument is convenient and attractive but also invalid. The internal trade in pornographic material in Denmark is considerably greater than any estimates for France where pornography is rigidly controlled. It is true that the turnover achieved by the Danish industry has fallen from the high peak it reached in its first year of effective legality but this is largely because greater competition has caused prices to fall. The actual number of items sold appears to have remained constant. It does seem that the volume of sales has now settled at a level considerably above that achieved in the years before the law was relaxed. There is certainly no evidence from America that the relaxation of the laws on pornography—whether in fact or in practice —decreases the amount of pornographic material sold. On the contrary, what does seem true is that although law cannot stop the sale of pornographic material, it can limit it considerably and confine it to those who really go out of their way to get it and who are prepared to pay high prices for it.

The anti-censorship lobby usually counters this by saying that the great difficulty is that one cannot draw the line and would it not be much easier to get rid of the whole business of control because there are always such arguments as to what is clearly designed to be pornographic and what is not. This allegation has had, of course, very great currency and is the instinctive reaction of many liberal people. They feel that there have been so many cases of books, subsequently seen as great works, being hounded by the courts, that it is much better to admit that this is not a proper area in which the law should operate. This argument does seem attractive at first sight but it has been well answered by Virginia Woolf whom Norman St John Stevas quoted in his discussion of pornography: 'There can be no doubt that books fall in respect of indecency into two classes. There are books written, published and sold with the object of causing pleasure or corruption by means of their indecency. There is no difficulty in finding where they are to be bought or in buying them when they are found. There are others whose indecency is not the object of the book but incidental to some other purpose—scientific, social, aesthetic— on the writer's part. The police magistrate's power should be definitely limited to the suppression of books which are sold as pornography to people who seek out and enjoy pornography. The others should be left alone. Any man or woman of average intelligence and culture knows the difference between the two kinds of book and has no difficulty in distinguishing one from the other.' And the novelist George Moore, who denied that pornography and literature overlap: 'On the contrary the frontiers are extremely well defined, so much so that even if all literature were searched through and through it would be difficult to find a book that a man of letters could not instantly place in one category or the other.' There really is a distinction between the two kinds of material—a distinction which has effectively been made in Britain with the Obscene Publications Act. The failure of the case against the book *Last Exit to Brooklyn* set the seal upon this. On appeal the law did allow publication even though many believe the book's literary merit is practically undiscernible and its prose unreadable.

In any case, even were all censorship to be lifted, a line still may have to be drawn. Many of the acts photographed in Danish publications are actually illegal in Great Britain and other countries. Is it suggested that unconsenting animals should be allowed to be misused in the way permitted in Scandinavia? That would be to introduce a new principle into the law of most Western nations—the principle that would allow activities in which one of the partners did not or could not agree—let alone any moral consideration of man's duty towards animals. We should in any case, like the Danes, have to draw the line at minors taking part in the photographic sessions. This simple matter has proved very difficult in the U.S.A. where advertisements like the following appear in the sex magazines—'Tammy is Ten. Unique photos now available of Tammy and other girls 8–14 years'. Even if we managed it better what line should be drawn—18 as the age of majority in many countries, 21—the age of consent for homosexuals in Britain or 16—the age of heterosexual consent in Britain. Wherever you draw the line you have to enforce the decision. What about the books which portray or purport to portray other acts which are illegal in many countries? Group sex—whether heterosexual or homosexual: activities which purport to involve minors even though the young participant is in fact over the age of consent; sadistic and masochistic material? The line is just as difficult to draw whether you admit pornographic material or not. And if you say that acts which are illegal may legally be photographed and placed on sale you are merely making a nonsense of the law.

But, say the supporters of pornography, this is a very valuable social service. It provides a much needed release for people who would otherwise be driven to worse excesses. As proof of this they point to the fact that in Denmark sex crimes have decreased by 31 per cent since pornography became legal. Of course this would be a very strong point in favour of the abolition of censorship if there were the remotest evidence for the claim. Once again it is a claim which has been given the very widest currency. In Britain the B.B.C. mentioned the figure on a news bulletin and pointed out the claim that was being made for freedom in pornography. It did not take time to correct the claim when closer examination revealed that the drop in sex crimes was apparent rather than real. At the same time as the pornography law was changed a number of activities which had previously been illegal were made legal. The manufacture, selling and advertising of pornography, voyeurism and similar offences were all abolished. So, as there were fewer crimes on the statute book, the number of crimes committed dropped. No doubt if burglary were made legal the Copenhagen crime rate would fall still further. What is interesting is that there was no significant fall in the number of cases of rape nor of assaults on minors—both being the sort of offences which the pro-pornography lobby believed would be affected. This is despite the fact that where a minor consents to intercourse this no longer constitutes rape, although intercourse with someone under fifteen is still a criminal offence. Indeed, there is reason to believe that the figures are even less reliable because the regular exposition of pornographic material and the general abuse heaped upon anyone who seeks to oppose it has lessened considerably the willingness of the ordinary person to complain even of those activities which are still illegal. People who can go and watch group sex activities of the most perverted kind are not very likely to complain about possible prostitution over the way. If one can watch films of homosexual orgies or read advertisements asking for partners in such orgies you are not so ready to pop off to the police when one seems to be going on in the next flat! It would hardly be surprising if the figures for sex crimes reported to the police did not fall and the fact that in the major sectors there has been no such drop may indicate an *increase* in crimes. Of course it was very naïve of anyone to suggest that legalization of pornography would have had so dramatic an effect so quickly or, if it had, that it was relevant, without seeing what the continuing trend would be.

Beyond all this is the 'porno is fun' argument. Pornography is pleasant and, if well presented, is a perfectly proper way of excitement and should therefore be allowed. Perhaps it would be as well to approach this argument with a certain cynicism as it does run totally counter to the feelings of the majority of people. In any case it is an argument to be met head on. Surely the exploitation of human beings which is an essential part of photographic pornography and the central burden of the non-illustrated type is precisely the kind of activity which Western civilization has been trying to control for generations. The nineteenth century prided itself on the social progress it made, seeing that young people were not forced to work overlong hours or in bad conditions injurious to their health. It is curious that when in all other spheres we are beginning to see the necessity of the best possible environment, in the sphere of pornography we are willing to allow people to live in a society which gives open opportunity to profit from dehumanizing one of the central facts of human experience. Nor is it enough to say that people would not do it if they disliked it. We stop even the willing from working in dangerous or inhuman conditions. There is all the difference in the world between allowing people to behave in private as they wish and allowing them to accept money for such behaviour in public or semi-public. It is the difference between fornication and prostitution, between a consenting adult and a paid accomplice.

The situation has never been as dangerous as it is now. By removing censorship we should not just increase the amount of pornography on the market, we should change its nature radically. Once it became a business much like any other, all the modern methods of printing and colour photography would be used, as they are in Denmark, to produce a product more attractive to a wider range of people. The stimulus of competition must mean that manufacturers and booksellers would attempt to widen the market opportunities and publicize their wares. Colour printing is an expensive business which the pornographic market has not been able to support in any country where it has been banned. The lifting of censorship in Denmark and Sweden has produced a totally new kind of material which would be developed even further were a large market like that of Germany or the U.K. opened up.

In any case, were we to remove censorship entirely we should have to legalize formally a number of activities which up to now most people have thought quite properly banned. It would have to be legal for people to perform sexual activities for gain and, as we shall see later, it is difficult to allow the sale of pornographic material freely if you are unprepared to allow live shows as well.

The protection of minors is one of the most difficult matters. There is a great temptation to take the easy way out in any consideration of pornography and argue that one needs to protect the young. Quite rightly this is not considered a sufficient reply to the legislation lobby. We could never use the needs of children as a standard for what we should or should not permit in society as a whole. Nonetheless, there is evidence from Denmark that the law has been totally unable to keep pornography from the hands of children and some recent American studies confirm the commonsense view that pornography can have a significant effect on young adolescents. Even though the dangers to the young are sometimes overstressed, their needs ought not to be forgotten and it might not be too much to ask the minority of adults who want pornography whether their suggested need is sufficient to outweigh the damage to growing minds that exposure to illustrated perversion might have.

In fact the present British law works quite well. The Customs are able to seize and dump large quantities of obviously pornographic material which no one has claimed has any merit at all. Although there is at the moment a case against this outstanding, the trade is limited to such few volumes as can be manufactured in the country or imported successfully. The illegality of the business and the high prices inevitably charged, scare off all but the most determined.

In two respects, however, both Britain and America could improve the situation enormously. The first is the misuse of the postal service for sending out advertising material which is liable to cause distress. Both countries have recently been concerned with tightening up their laws about direct mail selling to see that people do not find themselves imposed upon. In the same way the privacy and the views of the individual ought to be respected and circulars advertising pornographic material should be proceeded against. In the U.K. the Committee on

Privacy is looking at this very matter. If firms are unable to persuade booksellers to take their books because booksellers object to the content then there seems no good reason why they should force people to consider their merchandise in their own homes.

The second matter concerns bookshops which are solely concerned with the sale of pornographic material. The police know perfectly well what is being sold and the fact that it contravenes the law. Magistrates in Britain could have no hesitation in destroying large quantities of these books. Leave them their one copy of *Tropic of Cancer*, *Last Exit to Brooklyn* and their faded medical textbooks but get rid of *Sin for Breakfast*, *The Cult of Pain* and *Lesbian Career woman*.

In America the industry is very much more powerful than in any other country outside Scandinavia but by proceeding against the shops which sell the books and magazines and by tightening up on the postal regulations the situation can be considerably improved. Above all it is important that proceedings be taken against what is *unmistakably* pornographic and there is a great deal of such material. The situation in the U.S.A. is particularly difficult because of the very narrow interpretation of the Constitution which the Supreme Court has made. As a result the enforcement of any kind of control over pornographic material has become hazardous and this will be even more the case now that the President's Commission on Obscenity and Pornography has published its absurdly unscientific findings.

The Commission is a prize example of the dangers of pseudo-science. The Press reported its findings that only 2 per cent of Americans were worried about pornography. The Commission recommended: 'public opinion in America does not support the imposition of legal prohibitions upon the rights of adults to read or see explicit sexual materials. While a minority of Americans favour such prohibitions, a majority of the American people presently are of the view that adults should be legally able to read or see explicit sexual materials if they wish to do so.' All that sounds very convincing. The anti-pornography lobby is clearly a bunch of reactionaries, totally out of touch with majority feeling. This surprised some people because the Harris Poll in 1969, while the Commission was gathering its facts, published a survey which showed that '76 per cent of those tested want pornography outlawed and 72 per cent believed that erotica robs sexual relations of beauty'. Nor did the Commission seem to bear out the Gallup Poll which found that 85 per cent of Americans interviewed wanted more stringent State and local laws dealing with salacious material. On closer inspection it was found that the Commission had failed to take these two polls into account and had instead done one of its own in which it had asked one question: 'What do you think are the two or three major problems facing America today?' It was hardly surprising that most Americans put Vietnam, racial violence, inflation and unemployment, as well as student revolt, poverty and law and order, above pornography. No doubt the President of the U.S.A. would do the same but that would not mean he wanted no restrictions upon pornography! Yet this slanted evidence seems to have been characteristic of the Commission whose methodology was called by one eminent specialist a 'scientific scandal'. It must come as no great surprise that the Commission saw fit to make no studies on the long-range effects of pornography nor would it admit any evidence from studies already done. It had no in-depth clinical studies nor any on porno-violence. The Commission's methods were open to such heavy criticism that one member, who later signed the minority report, actually had to sue the Commission so that he could properly indicate his dissent from its findings and be given facilities for the minority report. As Senator McClellan said in his speech on the debate on the report: 'Never before, to my knowledge, in the history of Congressionally created Presidential Commissions, have constitutional rights been so infringed upon that one of its members was compelled to seek judicial relief.' Despite the obvious failings of the Commission's report which has contributed nothing new to the discussion, it has had an unhappy effect because its findings are quoted widely as if they have scientific basis and its views are used to brand as reactionaries all who disagree. Like the Danish figures for sex-crimes, no amount of putting the facts right will undo the initial harm which misreporting has caused.

Still we must be prepared to face up to the argument which says that there is no evidence that pornography does any harm and therefore there is no real reason to ban it at all. This view is the basic contention of the President's Commission and in the

U.K. it singles out the words in the British law which say that a jury should take the whole work and decide whether it will deprave or corrupt. Its contention is that, as nothing has ever been proved to do either, the law is a nonsense and should therefore be repealed. This is, of course, a more moderate position than that advocated by Kenneth Tynan. It does not claim that pornography is actually good for you but merely that its harmfulness cannot be proved. Ronald Butt's approach in *The Times* was perhaps the sanest on this issue. He asked how it was that one could say that continual contact with the best books and most valuable art would serve to ennoble a man when not at the same time saying that contact with the worst material and the most dehumanizing photographs would not debase him. A similar position was taken by President Nixon when he threw out the conclusions of the Commission on pornography.

The fact is that pornography debases the most important of human relationships, it makes a private thing a public spectacle, and replaces the ideal of total involvement with mere physical contact. Where art seeks to present the depths of human experience, pornography must display its superficialities.

Granted then that it trivializes—does it do any harm? Firstly, it certainly increases the level of tolerance in society. Exposure to perverted sexual activities, graphically told or illustrated, must mean that people are less shocked and more willing to accept them. Now society must somehow achieve a balance between the tolerance of those whose make-up leads them to perversion and the protection of its common standards and mores. Society can perfectly well say that it is barbarous to lock up homosexuals without at the same time saying that it wants to encourage homosexual activity. Such a society ought to be concerned at advertisements for magazines like the American *Gay* which say: 'GAY is for everybody. It means JOY! It is the doorway to new lifestyles that beckon to thinking people no matter what their sexual persuasions. . . . It is the enemy of rigid sexual preferences that exclude love's varied caresses.' Even more must it realize that pornography will add legitimacy to the fantasies of all kinds of people who desire activities we rate so harmful as to be illegal. It is unlikely that someone who never thought about practising sadism would suddenly seize upon it with enthusiasm through reading a

G

pornographic book. What is surely likely is that someone who had sadistic fantasies would find that pornography fed and encouraged them. So much of this material is designed to give the reader the feeling that he is not alone in his interests and his particular desires but that there are others—admirable people of taste and discrimination—who practise precisely what he desires but dare not do. Most will emerge only with more vivid imaginations, confirmed in their sexual slant, but we cannot rule out the fact that there may well be those for whom the confirmation which this material has given has been sufficient to push them towards acting out their desires. This would be even more true where the freeing of censorship would allow manufacturers every opportunity of modern technology to present the excitements and joys of each chosen type of perversion.

Psychological investigation has taught us that sexuality is very complex and that almost every personality has elements of desire within it other than the normal attraction to the opposite sex. We have to beware of thinking that these elements are more important, more real, and essentially more sincere than the basic drive. Of course we can emphasize and intensify the more perverted parts of our natures. We can bring out and indulge our latent sadism, masochism, or bestial instincts. Greek society shows how homosexual behaviour can be encouraged environmentally. If our society believes that the family forms the proper base upon which it can build and, if we think that people normally find themselves better able to be fulfilled within the marriage relationship, then we must seek to create an environment in which that relationship flourishes and which is fundamentally favourable to the order and stability which it entails. If, on the other hand, our intention is to be permissive in the sense which would permit the break-up of our society and if we wish not merely to be tolerant of the abnormal but to lay ourselves open to influences which will actually increase abnormal behaviour, then we must not only be perfectly aware of what we do but we must look for popular support which no Western nation has. As Ernest van den Haag has rightly pointed out: 'Everywhere intellectuals oppose and (with the possible exception of Scandinavia) blue collar workers favour censorship'. They do so precisely because instinctively they see censorship of this kind as a protection which society needs. Pornography must make its readers more willing to accept in themselves and others behaviour from which they would otherwise shy.

Well then, what about the borderline cases? What about the books with a serious purpose which treat of sexual behaviour explicitly. These must obviously have the chance to prove themselves in the courts although there is no reason why prosecutions should be frequent. All that is required is that society should have a way of keeping corporate watch on the activities of publishers who are otherwise the self-appointed arbiters of what is good for the public. If we abolish this right, then it means that we have removed from democratic and judicial control the decision as to what are ultimately the bounds of public decency. That means that such a decision is in future to be made by a small group of people who by residence and inclination are almost entirely metropolitan and who have a personal interest in publication. Of course a court, listening to expert evidence, is in a more impartial position to decide on whether the publication of *Last Exit to Brooklyn* is justified or not, than the publisher who stands to make a great deal of money from it. If, with all the opportunity for calling on any expert he likes, he cannot make out his case to the community then the community has a right to stop him publishing a book which it feels will deprave and corrupt just as it will stop him from building a new block of offices according to plan which it considers unsafe or unsightly. If he is refused planning permission for his offices he will be extremely annoyed and will think that the community has been unfair and that his case deserved to win. If he loses his case on a book then similarly he may feel aggrieved but the limitation upon freedom which is involved in either case, is a limitation which the community *must* impose upon individuals if it is to see that a society is created which accords with the hopes and aspirations of its members as a whole. Sir Elwyn Jones, the former British Attorney General, put the case to the European Ministers of Justice in May 1970. He pointed to the growing understanding of the need for control of environmental pollution—'It is paradoxical that, at such a time, there should also be a movement for the abandonment of any control of the cultural pollution represented by obscenity.'

We are not building an ideal society for the Lilac Establishment.

We are creating a democratic society, in which the blue-collar worker, and his wife, can have their views respected and weighed as well. It is no answer to this statement that we can leave people to read pornography who will and that those who do not want to need not do so. We live in a community and our inter-relationships are such that it is a matter of public concern that a business can be made out of producing ever more attractive material which exalts the very things which strike hardest against the central experience of man as a human being and as a social animal.

There are those, of course, who suggest that there are so many other trivializations of our society that there is no reason to pick on this. They point to the essential cheapening effect of the *News of the World* in Britain, of *Bild Zeitung* in Germany, or of the *National Inquirer* in the U.S.A. and ask, with all this going on, why should we think pornography important.

This is a curious argument because what it really postulates is that because there are a whole number of evils which we *cannot* control then we should not attempt to control those which *are* within our power. It also suggests that we confuse that which has no value with that which has less than it ought. The real trouble with the trivial is that it contains a germ of value which is then puffed up out of all proportion. This is precisely the kind of activity which education ought to combat. The inculcation of better standards and greater discrimination will help enormously.

Man's sexual impulses are not similarly amenable. Pornography has been the hobby of great intellects and men of enormous education and discrimination. It would be even more so if the market were enlarged by making it legal and thereby attracting into it the kind of creative talent which money can buy. It is surprising how difficult it is for the anti-censorship lobby to accept this. John Calder believes that a saner society with greater education will see a drop in 'rubbishy' reading and therefore of pornography. Yet that is really to equate two quite different things. Pornography can be made sufficiently attractive to overcome the discriminating person's natural dislike of the badly done. Its appeal, however, is directly to the passions rather than to the intellect and education has not invariably had much effect upon the passions. The trivial, on the other hand, *does* appeal to the lazy intellect and education can have a great effect in lessening that appeal.

It is natural for the permissive society to be concerned with the abolition of restraints upon pornography. It is natural because pornography strikes at the very values whose preservation the tolerant society demands and the permissive would sweep away. Permissiveness will push freedom to the limit precisely because it has exalted the virtues of variety and excitement to such an extent that it ignores those of stability and continuity. Pornography makes a change—indeed it is this virtue which the Danish pornographers continually push. They say that it will make a difference to a jaded palate. Pornography also glamourizes and encourages an attitude to sex which demands variety of relationships rather than depth. It is therefore a good deal more in tune with the fashionable trend than any idea of building something lasting. Yet it is on the lasting relationships that society has been built and society must have a death wish if it proceeds to allow that which must work towards its downfall.

What is essential, however, in the control of publications is that justice should be seen to be done. Now that in Britain and increasingly in other countries, the expert witness is adjudged a proper person to give evidence, the trial becomes the civilized way of seeing that the limits continue to be reasonable. Writers need greater scope at different times. The freedom required by Jane Austen is obviously far less than that needed by Mary McCarthy. The trial should not therefore be seen as a moment to claim that the whole business of censorship has broken down. It is the moment indeed when censorship is publicly being controlled. In the past publishers and popularists have done the community a disservice when they have attempted to laugh at the very idea of trying a book like *Last Exit to Brooklyn*. There was a very considerable difference of opinion and a court representing the community decided upon it. How proper that decision was is beside the point—what matters is that we have properly employed our judicial system. The only danger is that prosecutions will not be brought for fear that the intellectual outcry from those whose financial and professional interests are opposed to censorship of any kind, will make the authorities bringing the prosecution seem less trendy than they would like.

6 Pornography on Stage and Film

It happens to be convenient to divide any consideration of pornography into that which is printed and that which is enacted on film or the stage. This is in some ways an artificial distinction because, for instance, the photographic sex-book is so often the still version of a blue movie, and the fact that many films are designed not for public viewing but for home entertainment has blurred the differentiation which once existed. In addition, it is true that many of the principles which we have examined in relation to books apply also to the cinema and theatre. We have the same difficulty in deciding where the line is to be drawn, the same uncertainty about the corrupting effect of the material, and the same concern to decide how far society has a right to restrict the freedom of the individual in order to protect the community. Yet films and plays do also present special problems which must be considered.

Since the first moving pictures there have been blue films. Alex de Renzy, the most noted maker of American 'porno' films, claims to have examples which date from before the First World War. The medium is ideally suited for the purpose—it is the nearest thing to the real thing that is possible and the coming of super-8 and the imminent arrival of cassette television, mean that the market for home movies is bound to expand immensely.

Of course, the Danish censor-free society has enabled them to show and to manufacture blue films with no restrictions save those designed to protect minors. These films are usually made as part of an integrated manufacturing process so that the script and stills are used for photographic sex-books and the hundreds of feet of film used at any one session will be cut and various sections re-packaged so that a number of titles can be produced. In some circumstances the shooting of the film provides an opportunity to make further profits by charging entrance fees to those who wish to watch the live show and there is also the profitable sideline of manufacturing films about the making of pornographic films which are sold as semi-documentaries to be screened in countries which would not otherwise allow them. The success of *Sexual Freedom in Denmark* and *Censorship in Denmark: A new Approach*, both in making money and in further breaching the pornography laws in the U.S.A. seems to be the beginning of a vogue.

Yet, although the Danes and the Swedes are able to produce these films with minimal interference, it is the Americans who have been the main promoters of 'blue' films. This is largely because the much wider availability of home movie equipment had meant a bigger clandestine business even before recent relaxations in the law. Now that there is no restriction on the ownership of such films, business is really booming. Recent Federal court cases establishing this right are widely quoted in the advertisements—'If you are nervous about having these types of films in your home then stop worrying! According to recent court rulings, anything (even hard core pornography) goes, provided films are for private non-profit viewing.' Clearly this manufacturer believed that illegality *was* a bar to sales and that people's desire for pornography was not diminished once it was made legal!

There are still mailing restrictions under the Post Office Acts but these have been largely ignored, and recent changes are unlikely to work. A Federal Court has said, 'A person has a constitutional right to buy and receive obscene material' and as a result the film companies are busy recruiting agents to sell their wares. One manufacturer says 'Make $500, $600, $1,000 or more a week in your spare time,' another advertises, 'Salesmen wanted, earn hundreds of extra $ each week'. Another says simply 'Sex Sells'. Many use such propositions as a means of offering discounts to those who buy more than one film and as an excuse so that people who want films of deviant behaviour can order them without feeling that they have admitted their personal interest in a 'specialized' subject. Ordering is usually not done by title but either through sending for a catalogue or by marking the subjects which you want. Thus you can ask for Man and Woman relations; Group orgy relations; Man and Man relations; Single Gal (who loves herself) Single Guy (who loves himself). A 200 ft reel in colour will cost about \$30, in black and white, about \$20, and a few dollars more for super-8. As in Denmark the American experience is that prices are tending to drop as the activity becomes at least *de facto* legal, and more and more people want to enter a very lucrative business.

The actual photographing of these films is still subject to legal restrictions in the U.S.A. and it is more rare to find a filming session used as a live show for paying patrons as well for this would increase the possible penalties. In general producers are ignored by the law which has found it almost impossible to get a conviction against anyone who is prepared to fight a case right through to the Federal or Supreme courts. These courts are willing so to interpret the rights guaranteed under the American Constitution that practically no restrictions enacted by State legislature are valid. Most of these films are made under fairly primitive conditions with the minimum of equipment, using actors and actresses recruited through advertisements in the sex papers or propositioned on the street. Those participating affect a fairly cynical attitude to the whole matter although the women usually have a sort of half excuse like that given to one reporter, 'I'm interested in serious acting but jobs in the theatre are hard to get and I have to live.' The change in the attitude of young people and society in general to this sort of business has meant that film producers, both in Europe and America, can more easily get attractive young people to take part in the sessions. This is indeed one of the most noticeable differences between the films which are now being produced for home presentation and the stag films made ten years ago. The earlier ones usually showed that recruitment was difficult by using ageing and ugly models whose other activities had obviously been in much the same line of country for many years.

Whatever the excuse given, it is clear that the reason why actors and actresses take part is that they earn well. In Denmark the girls get £25–£30 a session and the boys, who are supposed to enjoy it more, get £15. In fact the actors claim to be totally unmoved by the experiences. One reporter said of a session he watched, 'During this whole thing one never felt any sexual excitement, everything seemed to be just too pat and clinical to be erotic or exciting.' The actors involved in this particular sequence said that all their reactions were simulated, for the sex act was only meaningful when you did it because you wanted to with someone you cared about—even if only very superficially! There is, of course, higher pay for anything more specialist than group sex. With amateur actors, very little equipment, and improvised studios it is no wonder that the majority of these films are technically very poor and certainly do not match the high technical standards of other forms of Danish and Swedish pornography. In the U.S.A., however, there has been a general tendency to make the whole business more professional and this has gathered momentum as the relaxation in the laws and in the general public's attitude has made it possible not only to sell these films for home projection but also to show them in movie theatres.

Before we look at the world of publicly shown pornography in America, we ought just to mention the peepshows which seem an almost exclusively American form. These are back projection machines which show a film loop similar to those used in schools for teaching basic skills. This continuous loop shows an act of sexual intercourse, or as much of it as the law in that particular town or state will allow. A showing costs a quarter and the increasing range of perversions and explicitness of these perversions is a good index to the fact that every month things become easier for the pornographer.

The real change in the U.S.A. has, however, been the increasing freedom which has been granted, particularly in California and New York, to those making films for public exhibition. Up to about 1968 there were certain cinemas which showed either nude films of the sun-worshipper kind, or more daring programmes which set out to present love positions or dealt with what was overtly a medical subject. These may have been pornographic in the sense that what they photographed was meant to be sexually arousing but in fact they always carried a sound track of momentous boredom which discussed all that was happening in clinical or psychological terms. In any case there were only about fifty such cinemas. Most major cities had a few 'nudie' programmes but it has only been in the last couple of years that the nude movie has really become overtly sexual—the real skin flick—and the number of cinemas showing such films has grown to over 1,000 with new ones being

built or old ones converted every week. A business which was
once concentrated on New York's 42nd Street has now spread
all over Manhattan.

These films are now treated as serious cinema. Their box
office takings are reported each week in *Variety* alongside the
normal products of the industry. Many of them receive reviews
in serious newspapers, so that even *The New York Times* carried
a report of *The Stewardesses*—a 3-D erotic epic which even the
most charitable critic could not have confused with a work of
art, although the airline pilots involved might have won an
Oscar for agility.

It was Alex de Renzy who really started the change. In
1968 he produced the first professionally made film which was
presented publicly without a fake medical soundtrack and
which showed totally exposed female genitals. *Time* magazine
said of this that it was 'bestowing the coup de grâce to the movies
last remaining sexual inhibitions'. They had seen nothing.
De Renzy has since produced more and more explicit films
with the result that today in San Francisco and increasingly in
New York and elsewhere there is nothing, however perverted,
that cannot be seen on the screen. So far the manufacturers of
these films have been specialists and the long established companies have not entered into the overtly pornographic market
but this is the major worry of the San Francisco District
Attorney who fears that in a desperate attempt to regain
falling cinema audiences the big film producers will pour vast
sums of money into the business.

This is, of course, a justifiable fear for were it to happen then
the whole situation would change. The money involved would
create a commercial pressure group which would be able to
combat any remaining restrictions. The advertising and commercial exploitation which such an investment would create
would, in turn, change the nature of the material produced.
The quality would certainly rise and with it the attempt to
entice as many people as possible into seeing the films presented.
Pornography produced with the resources of an M.G.M.
would no longer be something for a small and unhappy minority, it would become a product to be pushed with all the
selling techniques of modern capitalism.

Thus to legalize pornographic films is not merely to face up to something which has been there illegally since 1913 and which would be better out in the open. It is to create the opportunity for a total change in the business, a change which will be readily grasped in an industry frantically looking for ways to save itself. Indeed it is already true in Europe that producers wishing to make films of a more conventional kind are being asked to make a stronger version of the same material for sale in America and Scandinavia. Actors in such films are therefore faced with the choice of either consenting to do the extra sequences or of not working on the film. That choice is a very hard one in an industry in which more than fifty per cent of actors and producers are unemployed. The fear then is that the legalization of such films will have the effect of making what is already good business into an organized and advertised commercial operation, driving other films off the market, offering actors and producers little choice if they wish to stay in the industry, and using every means of public persuasion to increase interest in and attendance at film showings in the local cinemas of the commercial chains.

Already in Britain the industry is seriously worried because the gaps in the law enable film clubs, originally envisaged as a means whereby serious people interested in the cinema could see films not popular enough for general release, now to be used as a means of circumventing the censorship and obscenity laws. Like America before the early sixties, Great Britain has a system of self-censorship in the cinema industry. In the U.S.A. it was done largely through the Hollywood code by which most producers observed some generally accepted limits. In Britain there has been a British Board of Film Censors which accords a certificate restricting a film to an audience of one category or another so that children under certain ages can be excluded. The Secretary of the Board up to 1971 was John Trevelyan and his close and respected relationship with producers enabled them to seek advice on what would and what would not be allowed. The Board has been faced throughout with the need to keep in tune with general public feeling If they went too far then there would have been increasing demands for a much tougher policy with the possible opposite reaction which would have destroyed any kind of control. On the other hand, had they been too restrictive, then local authorities, and in particular the Greater London Council, would have used their powers to grant licences for public exhibition of films in the areas which they controlled in spite of the fact that they had been denied a certificate by the Censors. In principle such films could still have faced prosecution for obscenity but in practice no jury would be likely to uphold a case over a film which had been allowed by the local authority any more than if it had been given a certificate by the Board of Censors. In general this has meant that the film industry in Britain has had as much licence as has been necessary to treat any subject it wished. The breach in the wall has come with the establishment of the cinema clubs which have no pre-censorship and against which the police have found it impossible to act without a change in the law.

The films which the clubs show are very often of a kind which could be seized under the Customs regulations were they discovered during importation, and it certainly would be possible to prosecute the manufacturers were they discovered making the films. It is the exhibition of such films in a cinema club which is very difficult to stop as a recent case against an Andy Warhol presentation illustrated. In fact most of these club films are brought in from Europe and America. This is done either by carrying the whole copy of a film in hand luggage or by cutting the most objectionable scenes and importing the films quite regularly. The cut sequences are then smuggled in separately and respliced in.

Besides the Scandinavian producers, the Italians are very much in the forefront of the business which is for them largely an export matter as their own restrictions are more onerous than those of the U.S.A., Denmark or Sweden.

In Britain then there are versions of the same problems facing the Americans. But there is the opportunity to continue some sort of reasonable restriction which will be much more difficult to re-introduce in the U.S.A. If there were to be amending legislation enabling the police to prosecute clubs and if current cases against the Customs for their seizure of pornography fail, then the liberal system of pre-censorship with what amounts to an appeal to local authorities may well continue. It strikes a balance which gives any film-maker sufficient freedom to say what he wants without inevitably forcing upon

the public, toleration of the same kind of intentionally pornographic material which is increasingly part of the American
and Scandinavian scene. If the cinema clubs were controlled it
might encourage the Greater London Council to be a little
more responsible in their licensing policy. Their authority
stretches over an area in which one sixth of the population of
Britain lives and therefore even if they, alone of all local
Councils, allow films which the British Board of Film Censors
has refused, they can over the years discredit the Board's
operation. It is also true that there is a tendency for film-makers
to seek a London permission because this helps to sell the
film—it is well known that the G.L.C., although Conservative-
controlled, is less restrictive than the Board.

Yet all in all the existence of this appeal to the local authority
can be a safeguard against the power of the censor. It provides a
means whereby the public exercise of censorship can be
examined by an elected body and it is to be hoped that as such
it will become more responsive to public opinion than it has
shown in the past.

In America the problems are much more serious and some
action has to be taken if the large film producers are not going
to be forced by their parlous economic position into the business
of making overtly pornographic films. Now that President
Nixon has thrown out the report of the Presidential Commission
on pornography, supported by an overwhelming vote in Congress, we have the curious position of the executive and the
legislature being at one and yet being hamstrung by the
judicial interpretation of the Constitution. In these circumstances it may be that discriminatory tax laws are the
only way to restrict the growing business and discourage the
big operators from moving from legitimate film-making to
pornography. Such laws, coupled with a much tighter control
of sending pornographic material by mail would mean that,
although it would not be illegal to possess such material, it
would be extremely expensive to show it publicly or distribute
it. If at the same time it proves possible to continue restricting
the making of such films and possibly tightening control of
advertising which encourages people to send pornography
through the mail, then the present upsurge can be kept within
bounds and most 'sex' cinemas can be made uneconomic.

This would of course be an unsatisfactory way of containing the situation and is only suggested because of recent judgements' odd interpretation of the Constitution. Ideally a public system of censorship akin to that operating in Britain would not only mean that the film industry and its operatives were saved from death by pornography, but it would also begin to establish some way in which the community could properly take its part in deciding the standards which corporately it wished to uphold. Such a defined structure does have a number of advantages. It cuts out the maverick operation of laws in local jurisdiction. There would be no reason for the kind of infringement of personal liberty which was seen in Fulton County, Georgia when the police took photographs of the audience which had gathered to watch Andy Warhol's *Lonesome Cowboy* in order to be able to identify 'notorious homosexuals'. In fact there was a Unitarian minister in the cinema who has taken the case to the Supreme Court demanding that the photographs be destroyed. Such local situations are bound to arise in a country with the tradition of regional independence which is America's, but a national censorship system would expose such anomalies for what they are, whereas at present they can so often be excused by a population frustrated in its belief that the wishes of the overwhelming majority are being thwarted by an interpretation of the Constitution which was never envisaged by those who framed it nor intended by its amenders.

It is often suggested that this pre-censorship is a less satisfactory method of control than the kind of court case envisaged by the Obscene Publications Act in Britain which enables the operation of the censor to be subject to public scrutiny. As a general principle this is true but the experience of the operation of the British Board of Film Censors is such that, provided that the industry has confidence in the Board, it is much more helpful for producers to discuss problems in their scripts or realization while making the film, rather than have it banned or cut to pieces afterwards. The creation of a film, despite the current hang-up on directors doing their thing, is a corporate affair and the introduction of advice from the Censor is not therefore unacceptable. Writing a book is much more exclusive and personal and it would be inappropriate to have other than post-publication action.

That some action is necessary is made the more obvious by the technical advances in cassette television in the last three or four years. Just as the invention of the printing press was the change in technology which first necessitated censorship on grounds of obscenity, so the coming of the TV cassette poses new problems to be tackled. There are now five major cassette TV systems which are being or are about to be marketed in Europe and America. Three operate with a kind of cassetted video-tape and can be used for recording as well as playing and two others, one using film and the other a polythene and laser-beam combination will merely play the programme of your choice over the TV set in your home but cannot be used to record networked shows as well. Whichever system wins in the end there is no doubt that a revolution in communication is on the way. People will be able to choose their own programmes from a catalogue of films to hire or buy. Hoteliers and publicans will be able to present a special television programme which customers cannot get at home and which will then be a selling point just as cabarets, drag shows and talent competitions are today. Yet it will be so much simpler and yet on so much wider a scale that we ought to watch carefully how the industry expects the system to develop. The reputable hardware manufacturers naturally see the development coming first in education and industrial training and then in the home, particularly where people already hire their television set—as is the general practice in Britain. What everyone agrees is that the home consumer will have to be sold on a series of programmes which he can get nowhere else before he will be willing to go to the trouble and expense of installing the equipment and hiring or buying the cassettes. The major companies expect this to happen when he wishes to undertake an educational or semi-educational course; perhaps it will be a series leading to an external degree or professional qualification, perhaps a foreign language course, or even just one to improve his golf. Whichever it is, this is the make or break point not only for cassette TV in general but for each particular system. Given the huge sums which are already being ploughed into these systems, there will very soon come a time when the manufacturers will be desperate for any programmes which will encourage people to buy their hardware in preference to another system.

They will also have an increasing general concern for the expansion of the idea of cassette TV itself. At this point it is worth looking at the operation of some of the less reputable film-makers.

These are unconnected with the manufacturers of the hardware systems but they see in the expansion of the cassette-TV concept a whole new market for pornographic films. They have none of the problems of the legitimate film-makers who so far have been unable to work out an agreement with the unions on their payments and rights in cassette TV. Their films are all ready for transcription into the new medium. Even if the hardware manufacturers do not themselves take part in the operation, there is no reason why, in most of the systems, they should not produce their own cassettes. The market opportunities would be enormous. Up to now home movies have depended upon the purchase of a projector and screen. This has been an inhibiting factor, particularly in Europe where the fashion for gadgets in the home is less prevalent than in the U.S.A. The great advantage of the cassette TV is that it is either actually built into the TV or connected to it and it is therefore merely an extension of an already accepted article of furniture. There is thus no reason to doubt that, just as colour sets are rapidly replacing black and white, so sets with this added dimension will soon be the order of the day. With this enormous market opening up it is not surprising that the Japanese in particular are making huge quantities of pornographic films ready for exporting into Europe and America. The vast investment which is being put into cassette TV, the competition which is bound to be enormous, the fact that no manufacturer of a video-tape system can effectively inhibit other firms from producing material for his hardware, and the particular advantages of pornographic material as providing the reason to buy or hire one of the new systems—all these factors lead one to fear that we shall be faced, not with a decreasing business in such material, but with a well-financed international operation designed to sell pornographic films for home viewing. Such a situation can only be avoided if the legislative changes necessary in Europe and the U.S.A. are taken now so that the marketing operation is never created. It will be much more difficult to deal with the situation once there are large commercial interests involved. What is certain is that society will insist that something would have to be done, for example, to protect minors; it would lead to growing demands from the TV companies to screen such programmes, as it would seem illogical that people could watch a pornographic film on their TV set but not if it were diffused from a TV station; above all it would provide a market large and lucrative enough to ensure that the films would be technically excellent, well advertised, and cunningly justified. Pornography would have become a part, and an ugly part, of the way of life of all, whether they wanted it or not.

The case is, of course, quite different when we consider the live theatre. This is by definition a minority entertainment. People who go to see a play are generally perfectly aware of what they are going to see and the number of theatres is small enough for there to be some reasonable hope of restricting the audience to adults. It is therefore natural that we should accept very much greater freedom in the theatre than elsewhere. Minors can be protected and advertising matter restricted. The whole problem must therefore centre round where you draw the line. Kenneth Tynan in *Oh! Calcutta!* has made a great song and dance by going as far as either the American or British laws would let him. In the U.S.A. it was decided that as acts of sexual intercourse and sodomy did not actually take place on the stage but were merely mimed, it could continue. In Britain the Director of Public Prosecutions decided that no case could be sustained in the courts under the Obscene Publications Act. In this situation the American case was much more acceptable. At least it was argued out in court and people could see exactly what the law provided. It may be that the law is not restrictive enough but in Britain, the effect of abolishing the censorship powers of the Lord Chamberlain, has been to give the Director of Public Prosecutions the right to decide whether a case should go to the courts.

This arose over cases involving written material when the law was changed after Sir Cyril Black, a Conservative Member of Parliament, brought a private prosecution against *Last Exit to Brooklyn* in which the Metropolitan Magistrate used powers under ancient statutes to seize the book and ban sales. This put the onus of appeal on the publisher and created the

H

anomaly that what could not be sold in London could be sold in Wigan. However, the subsequent change in the law has meant that the Attorney-General and the Director of Public Prosecutions have the sole right in deciding whether a particular case shall be brought to court. This can in fact nullify all the advantages of the Obscene Publications Act which was envisaged as a measure to see that any book or play with literary merit could be produced but that at the same time the avowedly pornographic could be restricted. As it is politically embarrassing for any government to act in a case of this sort—it makes the Tories appear illiberal and the Socialists too conservative—this turn of events may make the Obscene Publications Act unworkable.

In fact there is a need in both Britain and America to face the problem of the live presentation which is merely pornographic. This is a major feature of the Danish scene and such presentations are advertised widely. They present in real life all those activities which are shown on film and in picture magazines. Like the films and magazines they become more and more extreme and fanciful as the search for novelty widens. All the objections which are sustained against the films and books are just as valid here but there is the additionally acute problem of the great shortage of work on the stage in most European countries which is paralleled in the U.S.A. Actors and actresses are put under enormous pressure to do what they would not otherwise consider proper, merely because that is all that is on offer. At any one time, British Equity—the actors' trade union—estimate that two-thirds of its members are out of work. An actress's average length of employment is fourteen weeks a year and for that she will be paid £450. An actor does a little better. On average he works for seventeen weeks and earns £800. In these circumstances people are often pressurized into doing things they would never do were it not that they needed the money. On the London stage, many dancers in particular find that if they are not prepared to dance in the nude they will not easily get a job.

In Britain, Equity, while making no moral stand, is finding it more and more necessary to insist that actors and actresses are fully aware from the start what it is that directors will require of them. In the recent shooting of a particularly outspoken film which has been made in Britain, things clearly took place on the set some of which involved a minor and which were not intended and which neither he nor the management were able to prevent. The same sort of danger will be present in any film or play of this type no matter how high the motives of those writing and producing it. It is also true that a refusal by an artist to take part in a particular scene will usually mean that he or she will never work with that director again. The question is whether there is any really effective way of combating the determination of some directors to push back the barriers until they fall altogether.

There do seem two ways in which regulations can be reasonably enforced. The first is to deal with sex shows. Here explicit legislation enabling a prosecution to be upheld against a production whose *intention* was pornographic, ought to be sufficient safeguard. The defence would be able to call expert witnesses and the prosecution could bring in support not only the content of the programme but the nature of its advertising and promotion. Any programme deemed by the court to have as its main purpose the sexual titillation of the audience would be severely restricted, perhaps by the simple method of prohibiting total nudity and the simulation of sexual intercourse. Should a producer or writer believe that he needed to go beyond these normal bounds then there would be no restrictions as long as he could show that what he wanted to do was artistically necessary. He could call all the evidence he wished and so could those who disagreed. The court, just like a public enquiry into planning problems, would then make up its mind on behalf of the community. No doubt the community will make mistakes but they will be public mistakes and as such they will point their lesson. In this way the presentation of pornographic material will not become the way to quick riches for the unscrupulous, nor will the genuine artist be denied the right to his freedom. Instead he will be protected from those whose search for total freedom is motivated more by their financial than their literary interests.

7 Television

The position of the writer or producer of a stage play is, of course, very different from that of the television writer and producer. The freedom given by an audience aware of what they have come to see must be very much greater than that accorded to a medium which is watched relatively indiscriminately.

Television is beamed into the homes of a nation and throughout the world, governments have always considered that special measures needed to be taken to control such a powerful force. Every country has been willing to accept a degree of interference in the organization of television which would have been found quite intolerable were it suggested for the Press. In Britain the two broadcasting authorities operate under statutes which considerably restrict their freedom of action and both bodies, appointed by the government, have a censorship function. In France, successive governments of all political persuasions have used their powers to control the radio and television system—O.R.T.F.—and to see to it that changes in personnel ensue if their desires are not carried out. Only in the United States do television companies have freedom from government interference comparable to that enjoyed by the Press and there, of course, they have to contend instead with the views of the advertisers who sponsor the shows.

Obviously the very nature of the medium dictates that it can and should be treated rather differently from other methods of communication. Government action comes in right at the start with the allocation of channels and, as these are limited, with the choice of those who should use them. The previous experience with wireless set the pattern in European countries for state-owned corporations providing a service in return for a licence fee. Commercial television has come later and indeed is only fully operative in Britain and Germany; elsewhere there have been a grudging few moments of advertising allowed in

France while none is allowed in Sweden, Denmark, or Italy.

Now it is true that technological limitations do in fact mean that television is a community service in a way which is true of no other communication medium. The audience must be defined as a mass audience simply because there is such a limited alternative choice. Where there is a commercial station then the needs of the advertisers will demand the highest audience ratings possible and this competition will certainly also affect the non-commercial chain in its attempts to attract enough alternative viewers. Even without such competition, the non-commercial companies are bound to accept that their prime duty is to the majority of their audience who may well have little alternative if they have no interest in the highbrow fare which is being provided. This must mean that the minority tastes are everywhere pushed into times of the day which are not popular viewing periods and where there is no reason to believe that audiences will be lost or the interests of the majority unduly disturbed. Any variation from this pattern can really only be achieved by the philanthropic efforts of educational stations in the U.S.A. or subsidy of the minority from licence fees as operated by B.B.C. 2 in the United Kingdom.

Basically, however, television is a mass medium, reaching into the homes of most of the nation and being the largest leisure-time activity of the majority. The pattern is similar all over Europe and America. Television is watched most by children, the middle-aged and the old and least by young adults. The lower the socio-economic group the more television is watched and the less control exercised over what is seen. In general this means that the less literate the family, the more hours of television the children are allowed.

Now all this has had some extremely fundamental effects. It has opened the minds of people to the world outside to an unparalleled extent. People whose reading habits are very limited and whose earning capacity is low, have a remarkable opportunity to see places and people and hear views and arguments which would never have been available to them in the pre-television era. This is something which is so often left unstressed by those who would attack the standards of television or its effect on reading or family life. Teachers dealing with children of less-educated families find in television the centre of a good deal of their classwork as it has become the children's one common experience. Very often it is the most useful way through to a child for whom television is a source of real entertainment about which he is able to talk with interest.

It is within this context that we can begin to see the great opportunity that television has as well as its great danger. For so many their *one common experience* is the television programme. No wonder politicians, teachers, and parish priests, all find that knowledge of the popular television series is a most important way of being able to talk to those with whom otherwise they would have little in common. Thus in a community where there is little communal life, where the greater family has broken down into tiny, self-contained parent-and-child units, television provides a communal experience and in some senses the common language which is otherwise lacking. In performing this service it does, of course, exercise an enormous influence upon people, changing their attitudes and exposing them to new influences.

Television does not instruct, it impresses. It creates an atmosphere by its general tone. The medium cannot help doing this and it is no criticism to say so. Naturally in a free society the continuous presentation of news, views, comedy, and drama does not fit into a pattern cleverly and purposely manipulated in order to brainwash. It does, however, often have certain common features which fundamentally affect the community. Television tends to be metropolitan. Its values and standards are overwhelmingly the values and standards of the large urban centres of a nation. It is in such centres that the stations are situated and there that the producers, performers and commentators live. Nor is TV simply metropolitan in a big-city sense—it is bound to be influenced first and foremost by the mores of that part of the city in which its producers live and the attitudes of the circles in which they move. These are the views of Manhattan in general and of Greenwich Village in particular—they are not those of Rockville Centre or Bayside, Queens. In Britain it is the common currency of fashionable Islington, or the King's Road, Chelsea, not the attitude of Forest Hill or Ealing. This must have a distorting effect. The views of swinging London or fashionable New York are very much removed from the concepts of people outside but it is a difference which is rarely grasped by the practitioners concerned. It is not that they are superior about the gap or even that they strive to increase it. It is much more that they hardly know it's there. Tony Palmer, the ex-B.B.C. TV film producer, now a maker of feature films and pop columnist for the *Observer* newspaper, showed this clearly when appearing as a guest on the radio pop programme *Speak-easy*. This is an hour-long show in which a panel discuss things with an audience of young people between 12 and 18. Palmer's acceptable, slightly cynical, left-wing views were totally out of place in this audience. They were from middle-class and working-class suburbia and opposed him on every major issue, reflecting the views of the silent majority. What was significant was his enormous surprise. He wrote an article in the weekly *Spectator* as a reaction and expressed his bewilderment that these people should think as they did. It was not just that he disagreed—it was that he had no idea of the ordinary reactions of those outside the tight communications circle.

In the same way television tends to ignore regional differences. The national corporations—the O.R.T.F. in France, the B.B.C. in Britain, and the R.A.I. in Italy—are particularly prone to this. Even where there are regional companies—like the independent companies in Britain or the private stations in America—economics dictate that the overwhelming majority of their programmes are networked. Such local programmes as are made tend more to increase the importance and influence of the regional urban centre from which they are broadcast rather than reflect the attitude of the region. There is no doubt that the importance of Manchester as an influence over north-east England has been considerably enhanced by the commercial television centre that it has become. Manchester is the capital of Granadaland.

Television also re-defines the regions of a nation. In Britain the advent of Anglia has done a great deal to give a sense of community to an area whose regional connections were previously much more diverse. This is both to gain and to lose something. There is a stronger sense of identity which the continual treatment of television creates; but there is also the loss of some local characteristics within a region, submerged by the urban influence created by the combination of the regional centre and the networked programmes.

Yet not only does television tend to reflect metropolitan values, it also falls in its day-to-day control into the hands of a particular kind of executive. As the business is an enormous consumer of talent and is so attractive to the young as a career, the majority of the people who in fact set the tone for programmes, are young, university-educated, classless communicators. These are precisely the kind of people for whom the popular values and the fashionable attitudes have the greatest appeal. This must reinforce the natural tendency of a medium always hungry for further material to be on the side of the new-fangled. By its very nature it must be concerned to reinforce the contention that the great virtues are those of novelty and excitement.

So too, television is affected by being a visual medium. It is the visually exciting which it must continuously seek. It therefore must tend to dramatize all situations in a way which is unnecessary in print or on the radio. There is, therefore, a built-in problem of distortion. A few stray bullets in an otherwise orderly change of government, the one demonstrator who attacks a policeman, and the one soldier on duty who does react to provocation—these are the situations which television must use to provide the visual stimulus essential to its effect. Two examples illustrate this well. One occurred in the news reporting of the war in Biafra when children, stricken with hunger, were seen grovelling headfirst in dustbins looking for food. A most effective television picture which illustrated accurately the appalling starvation caused by that war. It was a pity that the children were in fact fighting around in the dustbins for sweets which the TV cameramen had put there in order to get the picture they wanted.

The other occasion was at a rally in London at the end of 1970 when something over 2,000 people came to protest at the Polish government's repression. Speeches by British politicians and student leaders were followed by a march to the Polish Embassy. The whole affair was orderly and therefore not very photogenic except for a minor incident when a Communist with a pro-Russian banner marched around the edge of the crowd. There was a scuffle and the man was led away. In that evening's news, the independent channel gave its viewers the idea that there were a few hundred Poles who beat up a protester in Hyde Park—such is the power and the need for visual impact. News programmes and documentaries need pictures to go with words and the demands which are made by this requirement do not always correlate with the needs of the particular news item. They also affect the selection of what is newsworthy. The medium insists upon the importance of picture material and therefore it is often the case that stories which do not on their merits justify inclusion in a news broadcast or as part of a documentary are put in because they are visually exciting.

Television is indeed a metropolitan medium whose tendency is to iron out regional differences and impose by example the attitudes of the urban centre. Its practitioners are usually uprooted from any community, young and well-educated, with little experience of the world outside television. The visual demands of the medium, coupled with the sheer volume of material needed make novelty and excitement very important. All this added together must mean that television is a medium which will emphasize and underline the changeful element of life and underestimate the orderly and the continuing.

If, for example, it plans a programme on that most unchanging subject, the religious life, it must do so from the point of view of crisis. It will look at the impact of the changes of habit or rule, the shortage of nuns, or the increase in the number leaving their monasteries. Thus the 95 per cent which continues will always be viewed through the perspective of the 5 per cent which is change. This had the double effect of over-emphasizing the importance of change and of seeing everything distorted through the particular view which the apostle of change has chosen. Thus, even if the programme ends by deciding that the alteration is a bad thing, it will normally have approached the discussion through the eyes of the suggester of change.

Now this would not be significant if the subjects with which television deals were well understood by the audience. If one knows all about the monastic life then the matters which interest one *are* the changes which are coming about. If you know nothing and would not have the energy to find out, if it were not placed in front of you as a programme, you will form the impression that the world is perpetually in ferment and that change and variety, revolution and overthrow constitute the natural state of man.

The new can only properly be seen in the perspective of the old. Its significance and its value are only really understood by those who have grasped the significance and value of the situation it is replacing. Television as a medium is extremely ill-equipped to present matters in this way. Novelty is its life blood, the excuse for its programmes, and provides, above all, the reason to tempt people to watch.

All this means that television is the most important way in which fashion is spread throughout the community. The fashionable views and clothes, the happenings and the people, are now pushed out hourly to the public when once they were confined to limited daily publication and to specialist weeklies. Where people once had to make themselves aware of such changes and fashions which interested them, they now are prescribed as a diet if they watch television at all. All this has been crucial to the spread of the permissive attitude and the reaction to it. Permissiveness is a largely metropolitan phenomenon. The demand for relaxation of the laws on drugs and pornography came initially from young people in our large cities. The challenge which they present is a changeful demand and their demands and ideas gain credence first in the very circles where TV producers and performers move and have their being. What becomes a commonplace view to them is naturally reflected in their presentation of news and current events. It is, therefore, not surprising that the effect of television is not only to spread information fast but also to spread particular ways of looking at that information equally fast. Thus the vogue in sophisticated urban society is transmitted throughout the community not with malice aforethought but by a natural process.

A good example of this has been the upsurge of student protest throughout the world. Societies as different as Japan and Czechoslovakia, university systems as divorced as those of Cambridge and Berlin, all had their 'regulation' revolt. It was not just that American students exported their home troubles to Sussex, the London School of Economics, Paris and Milan; it was much more that the mass communication of university unrest played its part in focussing on the issues and demanding a response from students. Indeed students began to look at their universities in the terms of change and reform which was the angle through which they were presented on TV. Students all over the world know that there is ferment on other campuses; the only news which came out of the universities was news of further disasters because that is the way in which television is forced to present its information. As a visual medium it must, even more than newspapers, shun the comment and get on with the excitement.

Just as students begin to think that the natural state of universities is to be in revolt, so all of us can begin to see all life through revolutionary eyes. We see morality as the New Moralist sees it, the traditional position is taken for granted to be such as the apostle of change indicates. We see religion through the eyes of the rebel and never through those of the constant. It is the extremist who characterizes politics and rarely the moderate. In this way the most important method of mass communication and mass education educates and communicates by continually stressing the forces of change and revolution to an audience which has practically no idea of the old nor any real understanding of what is being attacked. It therefore produces a kind of semi-education where people become partially versed in the new with no knowledge of the old and very little sympathy with it because it has always been presented by the people whose point of view is that of the importance of change. It is the drug cases, the illegitimate babies, the fourth marriages and the heretical pronouncements which make the news and very soon people begin to believe that these are the norm. These are the things which are done. With this the permissive society has replaced the traditional values which previously obtained.

This is, of course, to simplify the operation but not to distort it. The comparison must be with traditional means of imparting information and knowledge. Society once handed on the wisdom it thought necessary for the young to learn in order to be able to judge. Their judgement was not brought to bear until the basic information about what society saw as important was understood. The TV method is totally different. It sets out to imply a judgement on matters of which the viewer knows little, on the basis of a number of carefully selected facts chosen to make maximum impact. It becomes the vehicle of instant judgement and its operators must perforce see that the judgement then induced is one wedded to the new.

Yet television is not only a great reinforcer of change, it is also a producer of indiscriminate heroes. The television personality who succeeds is invested with an authority which his talents may in no way deserve. That authority will stretch to areas in which he has no specialist knowledge and where his opinion is only as valuable as that of any articulate person. Yet it is promoted and received as if it had an importance well beyond this. A good example of this was the coverage of the British General Election in 1970. On the independent channel that wise and well-informed commentator on public affairs—David Frost—fresh from his triumph of reporting the first man on the moon, was helped in his assessment of the meaning of the results as they came in by a balanced team of experts. There was the popular comedy writer, Dennis Norden; the American television actor Robert Vaughn; the Methodist minister, Lord Soper; the novelist, John Braine; the radical, Robin Blackburn; and the comedian and cabaret artist, Peter Cook. Apart from Lord Soper, none of these persons had any direct knowledge of elections, politics, the particular campaign, the party platforms, or the issues which had been raised. Robert Vaughn was particularly ignorant as he had only just arrived from the United States. Only Lord Soper and John Braine had ever been known publicly to have expressed an intelligent view on British politics. Also taking part were a disc jockey and a character actress. Every member of this panel was solemnly asked for their views as if those views had any significance other than the significance which attaches to views in general. They were commenting on an election which returned a Conservative Government yet only one out of ten was in any sense a Conservative. Thus such is the power of television, it could seriously suggest that a suitable and useful way to comment on the election results as they came in, was to gather together a panel of people whose main common denominator was their ignorance of politics but whose views could be invested with importance merely because they happened to be in the public eye in some other connection.

Now this is of vital importance when it comes to the growth of the permissive society because it does mean that the television attitude to experts finds itself particularly at home when it comes to discussions of religion or morality. Any one who is well known can in television terms be accepted as a suitable commentator on these subjects. In America and Great Britain, for example, we have heard Tom Jones' views on religion which were distinguished only by their lack of depth.

(Of course the Church plays into the hands of this sort of attitude and parades Cliff Richard, not as a singer of religious songs but as if his views on religion were *more* significant because he is a pop star than they would be were he any young man with a faith in Christ.)

It is fairly easy for us to see that this kind of sham expertise should be distrusted. What is less easy is for television not to invest the views of the 'personality' with a kind of authority to which it has really no claim. It is not a sin of commission; it is the effect of regular television appearance. People really do think that a person who often appears on television has an ability to judge matters quite outside his field. There is, therefore, in every country a number of people presented on panels and introduced on talk shows, who pontificate on every subject as if they had some specialist knowledge.

The other problem so often arising in the presentation of the moral issues on television is that those who are committed to the traditional codes are firmly written off as prejudiced while those who are just as firmly committed to the new attitudes are considered unbiased. Thus in a recent programme on B.B.C. television concerning religion and politics, Denis Healey—then the Minister of Defence—continually discounted the views of Lord Longford on the grounds of his being a Roman Catholic, while Healey did not seem to understand that he was equally biased.

It is of course extremely difficult for the ordinary viewer to judge the standing of a man and the authority which he can really be said to have. Like any mass medium, television makes that discrimination more difficult because it is so often concerned not to present an argument but to create a newsworthy situation. This would not matter except that such programmes are often the only information on an issue which the majority get and the views expressed are taken as valid because people feel that television itself confers some sort of validity upon them.

There is then this basic paradox. On the one hand television has widened the horizons of more people than any other method of communication and on the other it imposes the attitudes and values of the metropolitan young upon a whole nation. Yet it would be wrong to overstate the case. Much of the material broadcast has embarrassingly little content to impose upon anyone. The American TV companies must bear the greatest blame for this. In their desperate search for further shows to fill in the enormous number of hours which a great variety of channels are able to offer, they have depended upon set formulas—mindless quiz shows; poorly made cartoons; and purposeless talk programmes. These formulas are developed from shows which do work; there are good quiz shows, good cartoons, and good talk programmes. But once the flair has gone the whole thing becomes a sort of community patience, whiling away the hours of the day, and television is seen at its trivializing worst. The trouble is that there is more time to be filled than either the talent or the economics can run to.

It is, nevertheless, the total impact on television output which must be considered in the context of the growth of the permissive society. The television companies are themselves aware of the importance of this so that in Britain, for example, the B.B.C. has seen that as little smoking as possible is shown on the screen so that the habit is not glamorized by the heroes and personalities who appear. If this is a right judgement, and it would seem to have gained widespread support, it is surprising that the same organization has been so deaf to demands that it should limit the amount of obscenity and extra-marital sex in its programmes. The demand is of exactly the same nature and is different in kind from the considerations which apply to the theatre or cinema. The concern is that television's cumulative effect is to glamorize a particular attitude to life, encouraging people to imitate that attitude and, more often, to believe it to be a more real and accepted one than that which they have been taught or see around them. The example of alcohol is pertinent here. As the rate of drunkenness and alcoholism rises throughout Europe and America and people blame on increasing affluence what they used to blame on grinding poverty, the cumulative effect of most television is that no family with a life style worth envying could possibly get through the evening without quite a bit to drink. Indeed so much so, that the cut-glass decanters and the whisky bottle have become the easy symbols of gracious living for TV playwrights. No one is suggesting that characters on television plays should never drink. All that should be said is that it is very easy for the cumulative effect to be to invest certain behaviour with a glamour which invites imitation and to make it an ineradicable part of a life-style which is intended to be attractive.

It is with this in mind that we must approach the various attempts of organizations in Europe and America to raise the standards of television material. There has, of course, been increasing concern about violence on TV. This is often discussed as if there were some direct link between a programme in which a man hangs himself and the death of a teenager who had watched the scene and modelled his suicide upon it. There are certainly a number of cases in which crimes and suicides have been copied from TV portrayals. There are also many examples in history of people copying from books and paintings. We really have to be careful not to impute causation to something which merely served as a model. The boy might well have intended suicide anyway and have copied the method rather than the thought. The young criminals probably intended to do the robbery and the play gave them a ready-worked plan. It really is unlikely that the direct effect of a TV presentation is as powerful as the simplest argument would suggest.

What is, however, much more true is that the general values portrayed by television day after day, must have a major effect upon viewers. This is precisely why television has at one and the same time both more and less effect upon its audience. It has less immediate effect than the film or the play because the whole atmosphere of the theatre and cinema make for a much more powerful direct impression—but it is a single impression. Television, in your own home, has a less complete command of an audience overfamiliar with the box in the corner, but it has a continuing influence whose sum total is likely to be fundamentally more effective.

That influence works in two ways. As it brings its message right into the family circle, television can bring into people's consciousness views and subjects which would not otherwise have been considered. They may not agree with the views or like the subjects but the fact that they are often treated on TV is bound to make them more suitable for discussion than they would otherwise have been. This is of course an effect of television which can be both immensely valuable and very harmful. It meant that the sufferings in Biafra and Pakistan forced their way much more effectively into the homes of the Western world than would otherwise have been the case. It means that people are willing to be concerned about all kinds of things outside their own community. Yet it also means that TV can force a society to accept attitudes and views which in the past it has been at pains to exclude. The continued use on television of 'Jesus Christ' as an expletive has brought into common use in Britain a blasphemy which would not have been heard in any circle with a concern for good manners even ten years ago. Of course this particular example has come about partially because of American programmes and artists which reflect a society where the phrase has always been more acceptable. The question is whether the British society has benefited by this change. Does it have to tolerate an ugliness which it has done without before? Does the code of ordinary good manners, which would avoid cheapening what some hold as sacred, have to be breached? Is it inevitable that a society should have to lose its sense of the shocking through long exposure to that which once would have appalled?

In fact this is precisely what has happened in the Western attitudes to riots. We have seen so many on TV that we have ceased to be shocked, and in ceasing to be shocked we may have lost one of the most important human reactions. The cynic is inhuman precisely because he is unshockable. It is not necessarily narrow-minded to be shocked; it may display a real understanding and sympathy to be outraged by something which affronts the human dignity of others. It is, therefore, not a simple matter of dismissing the shocked as if they were reactionaries who wanted lace-curtains to edge their view of life for ever and ever. It may be true that those who would ask for much greater responsibility on television do so because they are not prepared to have the attitudes and views of the overwhelming majority forcibly changed by the ugly or progressive few.

A good example of this issue has been the appearance of a number of American left-wing militants on the British television. There have been all kinds of objections to many of the particular

interviews but one, perhaps not the most important, was nevertheless very widespread. At intervals in many of the shows
the guests use the expression 'motherfucking'. Now there must
be very few homes in Britain in which this word is ever used.
There are a very large majority of homes where someone using
it would not be invited again. It is ugly and, in Britain, at
least, it is shocking. Since importation it has been used from
time to time by other 'forthright' performers. The word is now
less shocking because millions of people have been forced to
allow into their homes entertainers who have used it. Is there
any redeeming social reason why Britain should have to accept
this additional ugliness? The British Government would not
allow an alien to enter Britain and build an ugly building,
or disfigure a National Park. He would be controlled by planning acts designed specifically to preserve that very subjective
and often élitist quality—beauty. Is it not then the least that a
society can demand of television, that it faces up to its effect of
making acceptable that which was previously unacceptable.
It is, therefore, perfectly reasonable to see that the generally
accepted standards of behaviour are respected. That does not
mean that no one should use bad language on TV or that we
should do a sort of word-count of expletives of various categories. What it may mean is that we should continually be concerned with the overall effect of TV programmes knowing that
if people continually drink, habitually swear, or fornicate as
a matter of course, then we all become much more willing to
accept such behaviour in ourselves and others than would otherwise be so.

The second way in which television can fundamentally affect
the society is when it goes further than merely accustoming us to
what was once strange, and actually confers upon a particular
attitude or idea, opprobrium or praise. Now this is doubtless
quite unimportant in any individual programme but it becomes
a vital issue when an attitude is so widespread in the particular
circles in which television people move, that they see no reason
not to promote it.

For me the most glaring example of this was the promotion of
a cause in which I believe—the abolition of capital punishment.
The B.B.C. presented this issue with no attempt to find a
balanced argument against abolition. Even as an abolitionist

I

I was struck by the fact that it was not the sensible opponents of the reform whom the B.B.C. invited but the extremists who looked and sounded so out of date that no one could take them seriously. In name there had been a debate; in fact the evidence had been presented totally one-sidedly, not once but continually so that the public could only draw the conclusion that the supporters of hanging were all unbelievably stupid. This, of course, did not mean that the majority of people were won over to the 'progressive' side—it just meant that they were encouraged not to voice their views because of the company in which they would find themselves. That is not a commendable method of either communicating or promoting discussion, whatever our views on the particular issue. The same sort of technique was of course used on the issue of coloured immigration into Britain. Television preserved an attitude of non-discussion until actually forced into it by events. Then those who called for restriction were presented as racialists. American TV has begun to present the same sort of problems. Over the months the networks have put out a view of the Vietnam war which accords with the views of the metropolitan liberal establishment but not with the majority of the people.

Now this is not to suggest that TV should slavishly promote the views of the majority of the population. It is much more that in a national broadcasting service viewers have a right to demand that their attitudes should not be totally submerged by the fashionable concepts of the few. It just is not acceptable that people should in effect be told that the mores and manners of their nation can be changed without their having any say. In some countries this is recognized by the fact that the State has direct control of the medium. In Communist societies this is accepted and even in a country like France there is considerable political interference in the affairs of the O.R.T.F. Obviously such a view is unacceptable to those nations whose broadcasting has always had a tradition of total independence from governmental control. Nor would it meet the case, for it would merely be to substitute direction by the elected establishment for direction by the Lilac Establishment.

What is needed for the better running of the television services are changes in the structure of the whole operation which will give proper participation to the user of the service. If ever there was a case for participation, it is in the management of a medium which reaches into almost every home and which in cumulative effect can do so much to alter the attitudes and concepts of a nation. Two things do seem essential. First there ought to be an independent authority, not controlled by broadcasters, who could investigate complaints by the public in much the same way as the Press Council does in Britain. It is not sufficient for there to be lay governors of a broadcasting authority, as is the case with the B.B.C. and I.T.V., as these very soon become so identified with the service they control that their first duty is to justify their servants. Such a broadcasting council could insist upon public retraction and apology for mistaken information at a time commensurate with that when the original information was given. In this way the viewer, who has at the moment no redress outside the libel courts, could ensure that he has the same protection as the newspaper reader. He would have the advantages both of the letter to the editor and of a Press Council. In setting up the Broadcasting Council it would be important to take into account the tendency which television has to become too metropolitan so that members from outside the main urban areas would be vital. The same care should be taken in the second part of this re-structuring, which would be to extend to other countries the advisory arrangements which exist in Denmark. There every aspect of television is continually reviewed by advisory bodies set up quite independently of the Danish Broadcasting Authority. They fix their own meetings, call their own evidence, and produce their own reports. This is a much more satisfactory way of seeing that the public is involved than the pathetic and undemocratic British equivalents which are advisory bodies actually chosen by the programme-makers—the B.B.C. and the independent contracting companies. They meet when the companies want them to meet, with such information as the companies want them to have, and they only report publicly if the companies consider that advisable.

In America the situation is even worse as there are few proper means of consultation. The television medium is seen much more in terms of a commercial operation with sponsored programmes and a first duty to the advertiser. Thus even the rudimentary system in Britain has no equivalent. In fact society must see that it has as much a place in the control of television as it has, in the Food and Drugs Commission, in controlling the quality of what we eat; or through public enquiries, in determining the quality of the environment in which we wish to live.

Censorship or control of any kind of communication is bound to be repellent to any of us. Yet control by the community is surely better than control by a tiny oligarchy who may so easily, purposely or not, foist their standards and views upon the majority.

8 Drugs

It is a notable thing about the permissive society that it has arrived with so very little real opposition from the establishment. In general terms it has been a walkover and although Western attitudes of authority have not changed rapidly enough for the permissive hawks, they have, nonetheless, changed much more quickly than might have been expected. In a society still justified by the remnants of nineteenth-century liberalism, mixed with a little democratic socialism, and topped with the trappings of religion, there really was no relevant cohesive theory of the community which could provide the basis for opposition. Society had lost its nerve. Perhaps it had no right to uphold communal standards, to call the few to account in order to protect the many, to remind the new heroes that they had responsibilities towards their followers and their fans. It was easy to capitulate when the ground on which society had taken its stand was so uncertain and when its position was more one of habit than of real and lively belief. It took a new kind of challenge to force society to react decisively. It was the coming of the drug epidemic which was no respecter of class or colour, and which seemed essentially associated with forces out to destroy everything recognizable in the community—it was this that first pushed authority into a real assessment of the demands it could properly make upon the citizens which had given it power.

At first it was quite convenient to dismiss the challenge, on the basis that it was merely one aspect of the problem of dependence. We were living in an increasingly hectic society and it was therefore natural that more and more people would look to all kinds of artificial stimulants and comforters in order to come to terms with the pace of life. It was pointed out that alongside the growing problem of drug abuse there was the much vaster one of drug misuse with the millions of pills being swallowed by middle-aged people all over Europe and America to make them sleep, to wake them up, to tranquillize and then to make them sleep again. There was also the matter of alcoholism which for the first time was seen as a disease afflicting three million people in the U.S.A. and half a million in the United Kingdom. There were those who thought that the growing incidence of drug abuse was no more dangerous than this and that cannabis appeared much less dangerous. They also believed that it was a fad which might be expected to pass when the particular fashions in pop music and mod clothes passed. It was only when the enormous increase in the number of addicts became apparent, that the community woke up to the fact that it was faced with a problem which it had very little idea how to tackle. Instinctively, however, it saw this as a threat to its whole existence and, as so often, the instinctive solutions which it proposed were almost all wholly bad.

With no real attempt to analyse the reason for addiction and with a readiness to draw unacceptable parallels from other societies and other situations, the great clampdown began. In the United States and in Europe every possible penal sanction was imposed to try and stop the pushers and to restrict the use of drugs. The primary aim was to contain the menace and only secondarily was there any question of curing the addicts. Such cures as were attempted were almost all concerned solely with the addict's direct physical dependence and hardly any consideration given to why he was on the drug at all. A whole mythology of drug addiction grew up. The villain was the pusher whose purpose was to find new suckers to whom he would sell his wares which he was himself too smart to use. The argument was—catch the pushers and stop the supply, and all will be well. In the U.S.A. the French provided another good villain. They were not co-operating properly in the battle against the supplier who brought the stuff through France from the East and all kinds of savage retaliatory embargoes were suggested to stop this source of supply.

In Britain the authorities were anxious to show that they had profited from the experience of the U.S.A. This led to taking a number of unjustifiable inferences from the American scene. It was too late when they found that these did not have the direct application which they might suggest. In Sweden, the early clampdown was followed by a very liberal period which was so disastrous that they soon returned to a much tougher policy. In the Communist countries and the rest of Europe, governments have tended to impose or to bring up to date severe penalties for drug-trafficking and possession and then stand baffled as the wave of drug-taking has hit them. The inability of any government to deal with the problem reminds one of the effects of the Black Death—countries do what they have to do but actually hold out no real hope of stopping the menace. It is interesting too that, however permissive an attitude people take on other issues, there are many for whom drug addiction is a major exception to their general view.

Any understanding of the nature of drug abuse must start with an acceptance that we really do not understand what addiction is. People make very simple distinctions between 'psychological addiction' and 'physical addiction' and point to the fact that habitual use of certain substances creates a dependence so great that withdrawal of supply has an actual physical effect—referred to as 'cold turkey'. This is true, but if taken alone it does not explain the nature of dependence nor the reasons for addiction. People can, in fact, be taken off drugs in a physical sense relatively easily. What is difficult is for them to stay off them. Beyond the immediate chemical addiction there is a much more basic need which drugs have fulfilled and which the removal of drugs leaves quite untouched.

If we start from the position that there is a list of substances which we can call drugs and which have a kind of metaphysical property called 'addictiveness' then we may go on to believe that if only we can keep people off these named drugs we shall be all right. In fact we shall have failed to grasp that the basic problem is simply that more and more people in our society are seeking to disassociate from it through dependence on substances of one kind or another. The word 'substance' is perhaps best as it does remind us that people sniff glue, burn crushed sunflower seed and inject mayonnaise in order to get 'high' so that the problem is not simply one of getting people off heroin or amphetamines and then keeping them away from them. The real problem is much deeper than that and we must start in a sense where the addict starts.

For him addiction is a statement about his relationship with contemporary urban society. Dr J. Denson-Gerber the American founder of Odyssey House (a rehabilitation centre for drug addicts), puts the attitude very clearly. The addict says, 'I am not an object or a machine. I am, regardless of how you try to regulate my conduct, an individual. If I can express my rage at the way in which you exploit me and negate my humanness only by destroying myself, then destroy myself I will.' This may be a twisted and illogical position but then it is the stand of someone who, in the terms of our society, *is* twisted and illogical. Yet there is a qualitative difference between his cry and that demand for sexual permissiveness and licence which we have considered earlier. The addict may have failed to cope with society or he may have refused to cope with it but in his condition he is stating a real need. As one ex-addict said to Fr Kenneth Leech, while he was working as a priest among addicts in London, 'It's sad that they have to go this far for help. I think "help" is what they want rather than attention. After all, if you wear weird enough clothes you'll get attention. I used to want help but I couldn't say so. I only got it when I became a junkie.'

This is not to set drug addicts up as heroes or to deny that fashion and example play a big part in the terrifying growth of drug abuse; it is merely to say that we shall get nowhere if we think of drug addicts as people who have got into bad ways and who need a little stiffening of the will to get out of a habit which they will drop once they see it's killing them.

Real addiction is not a habit, it is a way of life. The addict knows perfectly well that he is killing himself but that is part of the reason for the hold it has on him. One Toronto amphetamine user said, 'The doctor said I have a year to live. So what? What else have I got to experiment with except my life?' We can ascribe some drug use to the urge to experiment, but this will not simply explain the continued and long-term use of a substance which no longer gives any of the early satisfaction and which is knowingly and obviously killing you. Nor can it explain the sudden upsurge and continued growth in drug-taking by young people from all sections of the community in every Western country.

The figures are really breathtaking: 224 teenagers died of drug abuse in New York city in 1969. Between 1960 and 1969 the city had had 4,254 deaths from drugs of which nearly a quarter were in 1969. It is estimated that there were then 125,000 active narcotic abusers in the U.S.A. and perhaps half a million who were regularly using one or other of the dangerous drugs. In Britain *registered* addicts climbed from 290 in 1953 to 2,782 by 1968 and addicts under 20 from nil in 1959 to 764 in 1968. In America the problem has now spread to children under 16 and in New York 55 of these youngsters died from narcotics in 1969. This means that the probable number of addicts under 16 in New York is 5,500 and there are more than 22,000 teenage addicts. It is not therefore surprising that narcotism is now the leading cause of death in the age group 15–35.

Although this pattern is at its most frightening in the U.S.A. it is becoming the model for all Western countries. In Montreal they had 75 registered heroin addicts in 1969 and by the end of 1970 the figure had risen to over 1,000. In Sweden and Denmark the pattern of growth is distressingly similar. It is a problem which all European countries face together with Canada and the U.S.A.

There do seem to be three age-ranges of addicts on hard drugs. To each of these we can attach certain common characteristics. Most of our previous knowledge has come from those addicts who are over twenty-five, even though they no longer form the majority group. In one American agency treating drug addiction it was found that the I.Q.s of male addicts in this group averaged 114. Such people sustain a habit which in the U.S.A. costs them anything between $50 and $100 a day. This must make them by definition liable to continuous lawbreaking. Their lives are a perpetual round of getting enough money to pay for the next fix, having it and then looking for more money. This explains a great deal of the petty larceny, attacks on cab-drivers and so on for what seem to be tiny sums of money. The only aim is to see that one gets enough to pay for the next fix.

In this way everything conspires to continue the cycle of alienation. The addict has to take to drugs because he feels that he doesn't belong to 'straight' society. The drugs gave him at first an excitement, now they provide him with an identity. He does not have to compete in society or face himself and his problems. Life can be brought down to the almost primeval level of searching for the wherewithal to have the next injection—his only aim. In a sense he is not destroying himself—he has already done that as far as his own self-esteem is concerned. He is now busy with the single job of ensuring he avoids the withdrawal symptoms by continuing his drug ingestion. This age-group tends to be loners. There is no drop-out community for them. They have not replaced the world with an alternative but have opted out.

In the age group below this there is a much greater sense of community-loyalty. The eighteen to twenty-five year olds are using drugs as a symbol of their joint alienation from the world. They too are aware of the self-destruction involved but for them it is a way of avoiding reality. They live in a society which continually tells individuals how easy it is to solve every problem. The communicators present in encapsulated form all the world's issues and suggest simple remedies. The advertisers all suggest that a little of this and you will be a success with all the girls, one of these tablets and all your tiredness will disappear, while only a few spots of something new and every cleaning problem will be spirited away. We are a society dedicated to suggesting that the solutions to all our problems are simple, fast, and attractively packaged.

Yet our experience says exactly the opposite. Young people find the business of growing up in our complex world exceedingly difficult. It would be so even if there were many guidelines to help them. In fact we have insisted that they shall be helped as little as possible by removing the basis of parental discipline from family life and imbibing the progressive nonsense retailed by some paediatricians as scientific fact. We have created a world in which youth is so important that childhood is truncated, so that young people are supposed to be grown up and responsible while they are still growing up. We have given in to their natural demand to make their own mistakes and their own decisions and then we wonder why it is that they become disillusioned because it is not as easy as it seemed.

Again the strongest and the average get by. The former through talent and the latter because he is less acutely aware of the real challenges and the real stresses. It is the sensitive and the inadequate who suffer—they cannot cope with a situation which demands mature answers and gives them no real time for personal growth. It is a sink-or-swim situation with which we have presented them and these are the ones who are sinking. As a result they cannot make it in the society to which they belong and their answer is that society itself is wrong and ought not to be that way. The fact that their own alternatives may seem pretty poor and hardly acceptable does not detract from the fact that this is the age-group which Dr Denson-Gerber has said 'Idealistically confronts the adults, no longer by rebellion because they believe they have clay feet but by revolution because they believe that adults have clay heads'.

Now of course they ought not to react by taking to drugs but when they do we have got to face the fact that it is our lack of involvement which has brought about the situation. The loss of authority by parents and adults in general has come just as much from idleness as from any philosophical belief in child-care theories. Authority by its nature implies responsibility. To wield it effectively you have got to know and to care where your children are. How much easier it has been to accept the easy dictum and 'leave the kids to it'. It is simple now to blame it on youth but we can hardly expect young people to have mature judgement unless we have created an atmosphere in which we are able to hand on such maturity as we had gathered ourselves. In such a situation we too could face up to these new problems which are presented to young people. These are the addicts which really ask not only for our help but for a generation which is prepared to relearn the business of raising children.

Perhaps even more frightening than the growth of addiction in these two age groups has been the phenomenon, first noted in the U.S.A., but now spreading rapidly to Europe, of addiction in children under eighteen—even in those as young as twelve or thirteen. At this stage addiction is a totally different sort of problem. It is a question of epidemics. The atmosphere of a school or area becomes such that drug-taking is the done thing and not to do so means exclusion from the group. Children at this age, particularly in a culture in which parents have abdicated their responsibility, will take a drug craze very much like any other craze and it has as much importance in their minds as listening to the Beatles or wearing mod gear. In such a case the only way to combat the craze is to combat it as a group and not individually. It is this *group* which must be weaned away, and the attitudes and mores of the *group* which must be changed.

The addiction of all three age-ranges may take many forms but in general falls into one of four categories. The first major category is the opiates—opium, heroin and morphine. Before the Second World War most opiate addiction in the West was among those who had learned the habit in China and the Far East or who had become addicted to morphine after therapeutic dosage. Of course during the nineteenth century there was a good deal of opium addiction either overtly, as with de Quincey, or unknowingly, as with many who took laudanum. Traffic in these drugs in North America is a highly organized matter, the operation in New York being controlled by three or four major importers. It arrives in a variety of ways, generally through France from the Middle and Far East. In such an environment there is evidence of widespread attempts to push the drug and create new addicts. In Toronto, for example, social workers believe that during 1970 over one pound of heroin was given away in order to encourage addiction.

In most countries the addict breaks the law precisely because he is an addict. In Britain the controlled licensing of addicts has been the system since 1926. While addicts were very few, scattered over wide areas, and with no common link, the system worked well. However, the habit became a craze and the proportion of heroin users jumped from under 15 per cent of all addicts in 1958 to over 80 per cent in 1968; more and more addicts were young people who started for no therapeutic reason. Then the arrangements had to be tightened up and now only registered treatment centres can provide the drugs to listed addicts. This ought to minimize the trafficking in heroin which arises from over-prescription through doctors' ignorance, inefficiency, or wilful exploitation. Addiction itself is still not a crime in Britain, nor can there be compulsory hospitalization, although an attempt to provide for this was made in Parliament in 1970.

Most heroin addicts in Britain can be traced back either to a group in the West End in the early 1950s or to some Canadians who came to Britain at the end of the decade. The heroin they use is very much stronger than that used in the U.S.A. where most addicts are probably not, strictly speaking, physically addicted. There is some evidence that specifically American elements of the heroin scene are spreading to Britain with the increase in the organized drug traffic and a certain spreading of heroin abuse to the rundown inner areas of London—a city which has up to now been free of addict neighbourhoods.

Beyond the basic personality need, the heroin addict begins by finding the drug gives him an enormous kick and he increases the dose to continue the experience. After a while he takes the drug because he fears withdrawal and because it has become for him a way of life. Many heroin addicts are also addicted to other drugs and such multiple use is an increasingly disturbing feature of the scene. This again underlines the danger of taking too much account of specific physical dependence.

Indeed one of the particular changes in the drug scene in the recent past has been increasing evidence of a link between the opiate taker and those who are dependent upon a second group of drugs—the amphetamines. Until recently these tended to be pill-takers and were largely dissociated from the heroin scene. Two things have altered this. The first is the improperly controlled use of the methadone treatment coupled with the effect of reducing the availability of heroin. The methadone treatment is a technique, pioneered in the U.S.A., by those who believed in physical addiction. This replaces dependence on the addictive drug heroin by giving instead injections of physeptone which was considered a non-addictive drug. The results in carefully controlled situations have been hopeful but not conclusive. In freer situations such as those operating in the U.K., where people undergoing the treatment as outpatients were often not under proper supervision, there has been a great increase in physeptone addiction. At the same time many amphetamine users have become addicted to injected drugs, using either methedrine or physeptone. The fact that they have begun to inject themselves, with a substance similar to that used by many heroin addicts, as a substitute or addiction to their own drug, has brought these two types of addicts much closer together. This becomes particularly true where the amount of heroin on the market declines sharply through police action or new legislation. In 1969 this was seen in parts of Canada where heroin supplies were effectively stopped by the

Mounties and as a result large numbers of addicts sought alternatives and, in particular, methadone.

There is some evidence of a similar situation in Britain. The establishment of treatment centres and the restriction of the legal supply of drugs to these centres, instead of allowing prescriptions by all doctors, has meant a decrease in the amount of heroin supplied legally. Previously heroin used to reach the market because registered addicts who got their supplies legally would sell off the extra, prescribed by doctors unskilled in the business, to unregistered addicts. Now, with less surplus coming on to the market, unregistered addicts have often changed to physeptone. Indeed the number of registered physeptone addicts is increasing every year and many of these have never undergone a methadone 'cure' but have just begun to use physeptone as a drug of dependence.

The amphetamine takers do, of course, range much wider than this. In Britain it all began seriously with the 'purple hearts' craze of the early 1960s. Like all amphetamines these, when taken in large doses, can create a psychotic condition. There are usually two types of takers—the week-ender who uses pills to keep high on his time off and the person for whom pills are a way of life. Those who take amphetamines can become excited and over-sensitive, even violent. There are also other pill-takers who take hypnotic substances which induce a sort of permanent semi-consciousness. Amphetamine addiction is particularly difficult to control in a world in which the use of drugs for ordinary medicinal purposes is so widespread and where the pill-takers have shown so versatile an ability to switch from one drug to another if the supply becomes difficult. In many ways these addicts are the most pathetic. They bolster up their feelings of inadequacy by injecting amphetamines and thus causing a short-lived 'rush' which they usually describe in sexual terms. It is an orgasm of the whole body—one addict said it was 'like coming at every pore'—and indeed some use the drugs as sexual stimulants. These are largely methylamphetamines or 'speed' and are injected combined with heroin and barbiturates or absorbed straight through the genital mucosa.

'Speed' does kill. About two years seems the average for the real addict before he dies of either pneumonia or other diseases, brought on by lack of food and physical deterioration, or from hepatitis caught from using unsterilized needles. *Time* magazine, in a feature on the drug scene in Canada, put the effect of this kind of addiction into personal terms with the story of the boy of thirteen from Halifax, Nova Scotia. He was led through a restaurant from the lavatory by police who had found him with a crushed Seconal sleeping tablet which he had mixed with water, heated, and put into a dirty syringe. Finding that all the veins in his arms had collapsed through continual injections, he had used the syringe on his tongue. Mere control of dangerous drugs can do little to help that kind of addict even were it possible in a country such as Canada which prescribed 612 million amphetamines and barbiturates through legal channels in 1969.

Even more difficult to control is the third group of drugs— the real hallucinogens, and principally LSD. This has been the most terrible story of all for it was exploited as the means of entering upon a new existence by Timothy Leary and his associates. As a result of the publicity, it is thought of as a 'soft' drug by many of the youngsters on the fringes of the drug scene. Its use is widespread and it can be made in the most elementary of laboratories; being colourless and odourless it is very easily concealed. Its therapeutic use has always been limited and usually questionable. Some psychoanalysts believed that it enabled the patient to return to the early days of his childhood and, through reliving the experience, find and destroy the causes of his disturbed condition. It is now rarely used for this purpose and there is little convincing evidence of any real benefits. As a drug it appears to have three major effects: it provides an appreciation of light and colour of great acuteness which is only palely copied in the psychedelic pictures of contemporary art; it also gives a feeling of ego-loss meaning that one's personality disappears and you are standing outside yourself, at one with the things you see; this brings with it the third effect—a claim to reach into new realms of conscious- ness and understand the meanings of things in an altogether new and deeper way. It is on this last claim that the real basis of LSD as a mind-opening, mystical drug is to be found. Most of its users see it as a short-cut to a mystical understanding of what the world is all about. What they see under its influence is believed to be more real than that which they can see merely with the mortal undrugged eye. This is, of course, the same claim which was made for mescalin and other derivatives from the Mexican peyote and similar 'mushroom' drugs.

It clearly does have the effect of presenting to the mind an amazingly compelling experience which appears to open 'the doors of perception'. What is however also true is that LSD can also give its users bad trips when they enter into hell and gibber and scream at the pictures they see. Under these influences they can try to gouge out their eyes to stop what they are seeing or throw themselves out of windows to escape from the images. Nor is the situation controllable once the trip is over. It can sometimes return months afterwards or it may simply return again and again over a long period. Even the apostles of LSD admit that it should be taken only in the best circumstances where there are others available to 'talk one down' from a bad trip. In fact this and other mind-altering drugs are extremely dangerous in all circumstances but more particularly because they have an attraction for those already disturbed and in need of psychiatric treatment. LSD attracts the psychotic personality—and does untold harm, often making the damage permanent so that the person will need continued treatment as his nightmares recur and the fundamental disorder in his mind is emphasized.

What is of course difficult, is that such mental effects are not inevitable, they are *often* present but not always and therefore many young people will not believe the evidence of doctors but prefer the advice of their fellows and of the gurus of the psychedelic world—the successors of Dr Leary. In fact even those who are not so dramatically afflicted are induced into the continued search for better and bigger drug experiences and thereby cease to be real members of the community. There is also growing evidence that LSD does direct damage to the chromosomes and has fundamental genetic effects. A good deal of further work has to be done in this matter but the indications do seem to be clear.

Much less clear is the situation of the fourth group—the so-called 'soft' drugs derived from the cannabis plant. Known by many different names, cannabis was not used widely until the fifties in the Western world, but confined to particular groups.

There was the jazz tradition of the twenties which continued the traditional use of cannabis and praised it in songs like Muggles; the Reefer song; and Sweet Marijuana Brown. Later there was the beat tradition of Ginsberg and Kerouac and of course its continuing use in seaport areas by immigrants and sailors from countries where cannabis smoking is endemic. The widespread use of the drug has been associated much more clearly with its place in the youth culture which the social and economic conditions of our age have produced. The publicity for it which has been provided by the pop heroes, who themselves took the habit from the jazz and 'beat' traditions, has made cannabis part of the whole pop package. Encouraged by the groups, praised in their songs, and spread at the meetings of the young, their festivals and their protest marches, cannabis is very much a symbol of the generation. It is not a drug of addiction nor does it appear to lead to tolerance as do the hard drugs. Its effect varies according to the situation in which it is used and the personality of the user. Comparisons of its effects are very difficult to make as studies often fail to take adequate account of the strength of the particular variety used. As far as is known there are no long-term harmful physical effects even after prolonged use of moderate doses—this is the conclusion both of the Wootton Commission on drugs in Britain and the Le Dain commission in Canada. On the other hand, Lady Wootton was careful to point out that there was evidence from those parts of the world where there was heavy and continuous consumption of the drug that it led to 'a syndrome of increasing mental and physical deterioration'. This is underlined by the fact that cannabis was put on the United Nations' list of dangerous drugs at the request of countries where its use was endemic and who had experience of its effects. It is still true that the most that can be said is that we do not know enough about cannabis to be sure what effects it may have—some recent work suggests that they may be more important than was at first thought to be the case. However, nothing very convincing has yet been shown.

The *afficionados* of cannabis say that it is a great help in creative work. There is absolutely no evidence for this although it does seem true that people using it have a higher opinion of their creative talents than the actual results would justify!

K

On the other hand the simple argument that cannabis smoking leads to the taking of hard drugs because most hard-drug takers have started on cannabis is an equally unfounded proposition. The overwhelming majority of cannabis smokers have no experience whatsoever of hard drugs and there is no evidence of any casual link between the two. What can be said, however, is that it may be psychologically easier to take hard drugs if you have already enjoyed the illegal effects of cannabis. It may be that for some people, once the barrier against drug-taking in any form is broken, then it is an easier move to other more dangerous drugs.

Yet the fact is that cannabis does provide our society with an enormously difficult problem. Its use is now extremely widespread. It is estimated that well over 50 per cent of college students in America have used it in the past six months and that, although the figures in Britain and France are considerably lower, the trend is exactly the same. The lack of direct evidence of its harmful effects would not be so dangerous if it were not that the growth of the habit is such that governments are now classing large sections of the population as criminals for doing something which they cannot *prove* to be harmful, while others are able to enjoy provably dangerous habits like smoking and drinking. Now it may be right for the State to continue to ban cannabis-smoking but it ought to be perfectly aware of what it is doing. It must, first of all, not rely on specious or provably false arguments about cannabis. If young people hear stories about cannabis which they know to be untrue then they will naturally be less willing to accept statements on the dangers of hard drugs. There is little doubt that we could have been more effective in discouraging experimentation with LSD if it had not been so easy for its supporters to cast doubt upon the medical evidence by pointing to the lies and half-truths which were trotted out in the case against cannabis. Nor are we on very strong ground to point to the fact that most heroin takers have used cannabis. The fact is that progression to heroin usually begins with alcohol whereas cannabis users are very often teetotal by habit.

Of course the illogicality is not only on one side in the argument. There are many who would argue for the legalization of cannabis and who would say that as it is obviously much less dangerous than alcohol or cigarettes, which we do allow, there is no reason why we should not be prepared to give people the right to smoke cannabis. England's Lord Chancellor, Lord Hailsham, gave the lie to this when he argued that no one was suggesting that we should *replace* cigarettes or alcohol with cannabis but rather that we should *add* to two dangerous substances a third one. Nor should we forget that it is only relatively recently that we have learned of the true extent of the dangers of tobacco. In the twenties the moralists who inveighed against the habit of cigarette smoking, and talked of its harmful effects were called puritans and reactionaries and criticized for being anti-life and anti-youth. There was no provable danger of tobacco taken in moderation and there seemed no evidence of long-term harmful effects. Today the puritans have been proved right and it is quite progressive and fashionable to talk of smoking as a dirty and unpleasant habit.

Another argument favoured by those who would legalize cannabis is that its use is now so widespread that the effects of making it illegal are much worse than those of allowing it. The usual example cited is prohibition in the U.S.A. which failed to work and brought instead all kinds of unlooked-for side-effects—with dope and gambling, gangsters and gunfights as well as making criminals out of ordinary people who were otherwise good citizens. This is an attractive argument. Prohibition clearly did not work because a highly vocal minority were not prepared to let it work. The difficulties were further increased by the fact that alcohol had been previously allowed and therefore there were many people who had become accustomed to it and had not found any of the bad effects claimed by its opponents. It was also true that there were many other countries which allowed their citizens to drink and suffered no ill effects. With this kind of background it is little wonder that prohibition did not work and we have become accustomed to accepting that its abolition was an unmixed blessing.

Yet the American community paid dearly for allowing alcohol and that was a price which has to be measured against the price of prohibition. Society elected to permit alcohol even though it is a deadly poison. There is ample evidence that alcohol *in excess* damages the brain, the peripheral nerves, the heart, and the liver. It is highly addictive and for alcoholics, of which there are six million in the U.S.A., the withdrawal syndrome can be 'fatal'. We continuously ignore the price paid for the ending of prohibition; the burden of alcoholism with all its attendant problems of death on the roads, vandalism, and the cost to the community of the working days lost. It is still true that on balance prohibition was an unacceptable alternative. The community would not wear it and the cost of enforcement as well as its impossibility was such that it just was not worth while.

We could compare this with the cannabis situation and judge when it could be said to have reached a similar state. It is clearly not yet true in Europe and even in the U.S.A. there are certain dissimilarities about the situation which we ought not to ignore. Firstly, unlike alcohol, there are no other countries to which the cannabis user can point which allow the habit. Nor is it true that cannabis was once legal and therefore people have got used to it and are loath to give it up. Perhaps just as important is the fact that cannabis is not as addictive as alcohol and therefore there is no physical reason why people should not stop using it. There may be a few who have a form of psychological addiction but these constitute a very small proportion of users. Lastly, just as cannabis is in large measure a fashionable component, a part of the pop revolution, there is some chance that its use may diminish as the focus of youthful revolt changes and its continuing illegality may encourage this. In all, the prohibition comparison does not provide us with the answer although it certainly gives us a warning.

That warning should remind us that the young people who use cannabis think that opposition to it is hypocritical. Even though it may not be logical to add cannabis to the other two vices on the grounds that it is less dangerous than either tobacco or alcohol, it is still true that the young tend to see another generation smugly prepared to go on sanctioning their own bad habits while ruthlessly attacking the much less dangerous behaviour of another generation. In this sense the illegality of cannabis has a symbolic importance way beyond the immediate issue. Like selling arms to South Africa, it is not just the act but what it stands for which must be considered.

On the other hand, Canadian experience suggests that cannabis smokers who are unable to get their drug tend to find some other replacement. This means that although cannabis does not lead on to heroin addiction, if supplies dry up then some users may turn to substitutes of a far more dangerous kind.

All in all this is not a question which can easily be answered. It is clear that cannabis is not a 'hard' drug. No simple statements can be made about its harmful effects. Its use is widespread and it has become a symbol for many young people of the way in which society is loaded against them. It is clearly less dangerous than alcohol or cigarettes and there is no evidence that it leads to the taking of hard drugs. Above all it may be a passing fashion which legislation will perpetuate into a permanent feature.

On the other hand we do not yet know whether cannabis has dangers as unsuspected as those lurking in tobacco but we do have some evidence from the Middle East that prolonged and heavy usage can produce an anti-social and unproductive syndrome. There is some evidence that those who have used cannabis are less inhibited in turning to other drugs if cannabis is not available and it is clearly true that our attempts to control the spread of the drug have been unsuccessful.

Faced with this siutation, there is clearly no obvious solution as there is in the case of LSD or heroin addiction. In Europe the position is easier as the habit is less widespread than in the U.S.A. There the reasoning of Britain's Wootton Report seems right. They believed that not sufficient was yet known about the effects of cannabis to make it possible responsibly to allow the practice. They therefore recommended that the penalties for possession should clearly be different from those prescribed for pushing and peddling other drugs but should still be sufficient to deter people from starting the use of it.

In the U.S.A. the difficulty of law enforcement and the widespread disregard of the statutes makes the whole problem more acute and yet even there it would seem wrong to make the use of pot legal. Clearly there are many who expect this to happen. We are told that the major tobacco firms have already registered suitable names like *Grass* and *Reefer*. Herein seems to lie the first objection to outright legalization. If cannabis is made a commercial proposition then an activity which may be harmful will become more than a fashion—it will be an accepted and advertised habit. This would not replace alcohol or tobacco but merely augment them. What if then we find, as we have with the other two products, that there are major dangers in its use? It will be too late.

Perhaps even more important is that it will give us another problem of socialization. We have only just begun to socialize the use of alcohol. Legislation to control drinking and driving and attempts to deal with the problem of alcoholism are now much more widespread. Yet alcohol has been part of our society for centuries and the damage has been enormous before we have got round to dealing with the problems. Surely this example should make us beware of saddling future generations with another similar problem.

So too the U.S.A. must look to its responsibility to those nations which have a greater chance of keeping cannabis under some control. It would hamper efforts in Europe immensely were America to legalize cannabis. Young people would see it only as a matter of time before their own governments capitulated and, fortified by that knowledge, the habit would spread even faster. In this situation it would seem sensible to adapt the laws at present in force so that a real distinction was made between cannabis-smoking and all other drug habits, but at the same time retaining sufficient deterrent to apply such restraint to growth of the habit as the law can.

This is, of course, a compromise. It will not satisfy the progressives nor will it seem other than a capitulation to the conservatives. Yet it will at least be logically defensible and will mark the fact that society does see a difference where a difference exists even though it still cannot with responsibility sanction the increase of a habit which does not advance the good of the community and about which there are many harmful indications.

This is, of course, only the beginning of a programme with which we must be concerned. The first step must be to coordinate our research into cannabis so that we shall be able to speak with more authority on its effect. The second step is to look more closely at what it is that has made this generation so prone to drug dependence. In this sense cannabis can be seen as part of the whole drug scene for the vogue which has led to its use is not unconnected with the general changes in society producing a generation disposed to drug use. We must not forget that many of these drugs have been known and available for hundreds of years. We cannot avoid the question —why now? What is it about our civilization which has produced a generation for whom drug-taking has become a problem when less affluent, more deprived communities have not done so?

To do this involves our refusal to write off drug addicts as if they are outcasts of whom society must take no account. It demands a readiness to face the fact that the sort of community in which the addict lives, and the kind of life which he has created will not make it easy for us to understand him nor he us. The very fact that he has taken to drugs is closely allied to his attitude to our society. He does believe that it has rejected him, just as strongly as we may see that he in turn has rejected it. In this situation we need the humility to accept that the fault is not all on one side. It may well be that the addict has rejected society for a good reason. His alternative life may be no better but the cause of his addiction may be a cause worth considering. What is clearly essential is to see the addiction as a symptom of a much deeper problem rather than treating it as the problem itself. In this way we must expect to look for a cure in terms of the personality of the addict and the society in which he lives rather than in some mechanical or physical treatment of his addiction.

One common element in all the literature about drugs is the obsession of the addict with his own personality and individuality. In many ways this is a dominant obsession of the whole of our post-Freudian individualist age. Our society is being polarized into groups and is no longer in any sense a community. We are increasingly aware of our economic, social, racial, and sexual differences and we are more and more worried about our ability to communicate across these barriers. As the family groupings break down into tiny units, young and old cease to communicate, and each generation and group identifies with its like rather than with its community. The individual is increasingly isolated, finding it more and more difficult to feel a sense of belonging.

It is little wonder that in these circumstances only the strongest and the least sensitive survive. For the majority the situation is accepted. Yet for some there is a deep need for help—a need which society cannot meet. In many the need will arise from some basic psychological weakness. The individual may have come from a desperately insecure family or no family at all; he may be emotionally inadequate or sexually deviant— whatever it is, he makes a demand upon society which the community should respond to and which in the past it has more readily responded to. It is the failure of the individual to deal adequately with his own need and the failure of the community to respond that drives him to opt out. It is in this sense that drug addiction is a cry for help. It is the demand of the trapped individual who, finding that the community has no place for him, has to show them he is important even if the only way he can do so is by demonstrating his power of self-destruction.

Not that all this makes it any easier for the community to deal with the problem. Straight physical cures just do not work. You merely take someone off drugs and put him back into the situation which has caused his addiction in the first place. Nor does it help to assume that the addict actually prefers the 'straight' world to his own. After all, he has chosen his own precisely because he cannot live in the ordinary society. Thus whatever the curative answer is, it must be found in some sort of community therapy which will enable the addict not only to kick the habit but to seek a 'return' to society by creating self-respect and curing the inadequacies of personality which led to drug dependence.

This is why the whole business is so much more difficult than was at first realized. Dr Ramirez, who founded the Phoenix House programme for rehabilitation of addicts in New York is convinced that 'the addict's problem results from a funda-mental but treatable character disorder'. Yet even this is too simple, for it suggests that the present society is such that individuals can properly be called upon to deal with the stresses it imposes and that those who cannot must *ipse facto* have a 'character disorder'. What may be nearer the mark is the con-cept that many individuals would have coped adequately in previous societies but that the particular stress of our present-day society is too much. This view claims that society is funda-mentally to blame in organizing itself so that it seems to exclude an increasing number of its nominal members. Whose fault this is we shall discuss later but in the meanwhile we must look to the solution of drug dependence in the creation of specialized communities where the ex-addict can grow to a point in which he can cope with society as it is.

This concept of a therapeutic community is one which has been tried with increasing success, largely in the United States. Organizations like Daytop, Synanon, Phoenix and Odyssey— all with their special insights and particular problems—do produce evidence of a basic scheme which does work and from which people go back into society able to cope with its stresses and strains. The sort of community which is able to achieve this is opposed in almost every way to the community beloved of the progressives, but is none the worse for that.

The first pre-requisite is that the addict should be given security and a feeling that he belongs. After all, one of the main reasons why addicts continue to take drugs even when the early sense of elation can no longer be reached is for what Dr Denson-Gerber has called 'the habituation to an all-involving life style that is admired within the addict subculture'. As an addict he was someone. He knew his rôle and he belonged. The one thing that must not be denied him therefore is a place and a rôle within a community to which he belongs. Thus it is necessary that the therapeutic community should have a hierarchical structure in which the new member takes his place with specific duties and responsibilities. He will find that his progress through the programme and increasing seniority in the community will depend on his response to the demands made of him. It will be the leaders of the community who, with the other members, will decide his rate of progress. The therapy will begin right from the start as he confronts his fellows and by statement and discussion he will begin to face himself, his qualities as well as his faults, through the eyes of the other members of the community.

Disagreement and unacceptable conduct are also faced communally. Most important is the fact that this is a community in which there are basic rules which must never be broken without 'excommunication'. No drugs may be used. There must be no sexual relations as those who are only just learning to be responsible for themselves cannot take responsibility for others. There must be no alcohol and no theft. Some communities add to these but most have much the same basis.

The key to it all is that the others within the community are also ex-addicts and all are continuing proof that the therapy works. In some organizations there are no professional psychiatrists or doctors, in others the professionals are part of the set-up and sometimes they are just on call. In fact the ideal solution seems to be to make them part of the set-up but in that case they must be accepted by the community because they alone within it do not have the ticket of admittance—they are not ex-addicts.

Odyssey House has overcome this by ensuring that in the hierarchy the 'professionals' are not automatically at the top. In their professional capacity they cannot be overruled by a non-professional but in the 'pecking order' they can easily come below an ex-addict who is responsible for administration or finance. This situation obviously makes it easier for suitable ex-addicts to act as bridges between the newcomers and the professional staff. One such individual is Alton Johnson— a Negro ex-addict and now one of the most senior members of the Odyssey House staff. He is seen as an ex-addict and therefore in a real sense someone with whom the newcomer can identify. He is black and yet he has succeeded—that is a vital piece of hope for any Negro who is just beginning to try. Such a person is able to act as a go-between and the newcomer, perhaps unable to trust the professional who is of another world, *can* trust the ex-addict. In turn, the professional can trust as go-between a man who has himself experience of the course and can interpret it in terms which the newcomer can understand. For interpretation is vitally necessary. The language of the drug sub-culture, its values and its modes of thought are so alien to many of those professionally concerned that an interpretative bridge is essential. Of course such a bridge has only a short useful life. The modes and views of the drug culture change. The ex-addict grows older and matures. Soon it will be increasingly difficult for the newcomer to accept him as an ex-addict and other people more recently involved must take his place.

The system is in essence simple. It is to take the addict and place him in a community with which he can identify among people whom he can begin to trust and then allow that community, professionally directed, to enable him to grow to self-respect.

This system does beg a number of questions. If drug addicts need a community in order to find their way back to self-respect, then it may be that the general community has failed to create a proper environment in which that self-respect would not have been lost? As widespread drug addiction is a recent phenomenon in the Western world, may the reason for its growth not be found in the changes which have been wrought in our community over the past fifty years? Above all, why is it that any non-addict who lives in such a therapeutic community for even a short time, comes away with a conviction that what is being created there is far more sane and provides a better environment in which *any* individual can grow than the hollow sham which we dignify with the name society in the outside world?

9 Meanwhile, where was the Church?

The Christian Church has always assumed a particular responsibility in the moral sphere. Christianity's ethics are fundamental to its faith, and Christ was continually and centrally concerned with the working out of the Law and the knowledge of God in the lives of men. He was, it is true, much more concerned with the sins of the spirit than with those of the flesh but his precepts and the subsequent teaching of the Church embraced the whole sphere of human action.

The tenor of our times has affected Christian ethics in two main areas—the first that of sexual morality and the second the social mission of the Church. Any analysis of the reaction of Christians to this new situation must begin with sexual morality because it is here that the attack has been strongest and where the Church's traditional position is most at variance with popular mores. It is also true that an older generation has tended to single out sexual morality as the key issue upon which to condemn today's youth while the popular commentators have chosen this as the best way of pointing to the irrelevance of Christian teaching.

The Church is, of course, by tradition, the defender of 'old-style' morality and it has been the ambivalence and uncertainty in the Church's reaction to the changes in Western society that have perhaps been the most unhappy of all. One must admit from the outset that the Church was in a very difficult position. It had sold traditional morality to a previous generation on what was very largely a false prospectus and its chickens were coming home to roost. The justification of the ban on extra-marital sexual intercourse had been the dangers of having an illegitimate baby or the strong possibility of disease. The taboos had been reinforced by reminders of the shame if society knew and the need for a woman to preserve her virginity intact because, when she married, her husband would expect it. The breakdown of the community and the coming of the Pill made most of these arguments irrelevant and the Church was forced back upon the real argument of personality which, although much more convincing, is much more difficult to put over, particularly when it looks as if you are only using it because you have been defeated on other grounds.

But the Church's position was in fact even more fundamentally in danger. Historically, morality has always been presented as a return from the giddiness of the new-fangled ways to the sobriety of former years. Moses' Ten Commandments were messages from the old God to a people immersed in the worship of the Golden Calf. Even Buddha preached a return to simplicity and 'return' has always been a central theme in the presentation of ethical views. Of no religion has this been more true than the Christian, whose emphasis upon the importance of historical facts and apostolic events has intensified the tendency to preach a return to former standards. The Cistercian reformers claimed to set up no new system of monasticism but looked back to primitive Benedictinism. Even Luther and Calvin saw themselves as ridding the Church of its new accretions and returning to an earlier and purer state.

The claim which both Evangelical and Tractarian had in common in the nineteenth century was that they were *recovering* the form of Christianity and their appeal was to a moral sense which recognized the concept of earlier and higher standards.

Today the Church has found itself faced with an atmosphere totally antagonistic to that in which its moral message has in the past been taught. The intellectual climate of our age, powerfully assisted by the forces of mass communication, is obsessed with finding virtue in new things. At its lowest this means that it is preoccupied by fashion and fashion must assert that all that has gone before is old hat. Fashion demands that we concern ourselves with the present. We must not look to the past or we shall not be suitably up to date. Nor must we look too much at the future or we might reflect that tomorrow something even more up-to-the-minute will make today's craze the oldest hat of all. Now of course societies have always been concerned with fashion. It is no new phenomenon but its centrality and importance is altogether new. The change in status is perhaps most vividly shown in the heroes of our time. They are almost exclusively the pop stars, photographers, and models whose existence depends upon mass acceptance of a vogue. The new importance of fashion is of course due to its vital rôle in the capitalist system. The selling of consumer goods depends on a mass market and mass production for that market. People must continually buy if the system is to operate. Without change in fashion many industries would be hard put to find a continuing market.

This is why 'new' is so important a word in the advertisers' vocabulary. Even the manufacturers of products which have relied on their traditional appeal to imply value and old-fashioned goodness will see to it that they inject something new alongside. Even Olde English Marmalade has 'tenderised peel' to make it more modern than its competitors. Old Quebec may have the charm of a '350 year-old walled city' but basically its advertising line is that it lies in 'the new and totally different world of French Canada'. Even Greece is the 'new' place!

Now in a society dedicated to newness and faced with a revolt against morality from the most fashion-conscious generations of all, the Church has a major problem of communication. It has never been one of the justifications of morality that it is new, on the contrary it has previously gained a good deal of strength from the fact that it was the ancient wisdom. It was little wonder that the traditional forces in the Church appeared to have no moral armour in this new situation. They often retreated into reiterating the position of pre-war days and using the pre-war language to state their case. It was not surprising that this made little sense to a younger generation for whom morality as the old wisdom was anathema. Some clerics sought a way out, not through the re-presentation of the old insight, but by a radical re-formulation of the whole question. They were faced with very little effective competition and thus the exponents of the New Morality took the centre of the stage. It is natural that we should look at these views with a certain degree of caution because they are postulating that the 1970s man has become so fundamentally different, that our whole basis of making moral judgements must be changed and become new.

Yet this is precisely what John Robinson and James Fletcher would have us believe. Bishop Robinson refers to Fletcher's

views as 'the only ethic for man come of age' and it is the continuing characteristic of his writings that we are now faced
with such a different world that we must produce a different
morality to cope with it. Of course, as we have seen, certain
conditions enter into ethical considerations today which did
not obtain before. Modern man can now have sexual intercourse outside marriage without fear of having a baby and
thus the Church's easiest point against this is now discounted.
Yet modern man himself has not changed. It is his circumstances
that have altered. There are major differences in modern society,
there are different opportunities, and different temptations.
We may well have to think out our attitudes to certain specific
problems which technological changes have made more acute,
but we really cannot claim that man has changed so much that
he needs a new morality.

To do so would be to go even further than Christ—without
any of the divine sanction which he claimed. Christ after all
said that he came not to destroy the Law but to fulfil it and it
is with the same kind of spirit that the Church should be facing
the challenge to traditional morality. Fletcher would, despite
his protestations to the contrary, throw out the Law altogether
and leave us to approach each moral decision as it comes, with
the benefit of but one Commandment—'Thou shalt love thy
neighbour as thyself.' Christ, on the other hand, did need two
Commandments and he put the love of God first in his order of
priorities.

Fletcher is, of course, attempting to create a Christian morality which would fit more naturally into the new permissive
society. He does believe that things have changed so much
that it is irrelevant to rethink traditional morality and present
it in a more contemporary form. He believes that the values
of today call forth from the Church a new morality which is
not lawless but takes into account the situation in the context
of law and the opinion of the great moralists of the past. This
position is difficult to uphold. If it is to mean anything more
than that 'once in a million cases the Christian has to break the
law if he is to be charitable', then it must mean that
law is usually subordinated to the demands of the situation.
This would harmonize precisely with the attitudes and philosophy behind the permissive society.

In examining the kind of moral problem which our society presents, Fletcher lights upon the issue of abortion and faces us with a schizophrenic girl who has been raped by a fellow patient in a mental hospital. The question is—should the baby live or die? Fletcher says that the rotten old legalists would insist on the baby's right to live while modern, post-Freudian, 'one-Commandment' Christians would immediately recognize the girl as their neighbour and kill her progeny. This is of course to say to the advocates of the permissive society that they are right and that their kind of love is all that we need. It is convenient, worldly-wise sentimentality. Now this does not seem a Christian answer. What Fletcher is really saying is that we should weigh the baby's life as of little import and it is in no position to complain—like the man on the road to Jericho, he can easily be considered dead, whereas the girl's father, the hospital authorities, and the man in the street, can drum up a good deal of public support for the raped girl. It is, in fact, not to apply the unique Christian revelation to the moral problems of the 1970s but rather to take over the moral views of the permissive society and call them Christian.

The orthodox position of the Church is quite clear although perhaps more rarely advertised. It would say that the New Morality is an old heresy under a new guise. It is the classic demand for Christians to accept the wisdom of the world instead of the truth of Christ. It is the final temptation in the wilderness —the offer of the kingdoms of the world in exchange for worshipping the devil.

Indeed it is interesting that the protagonists of the New Morality leave out the first of Christ's Commandments— love for God ill accords with the practical effects of situation ethics. It is this emphasis on the first Commandment as well as the second which marks out the orthodox Christian approach. Loving the Lord our God, not only gives us a point of reference in our dealings with human beings—it universalizes our decision-making. We cease only to be concerned with the schizophrenic girl. We have to be concerned with all God's creation. With the child who is to be born and with others for whom this abortion may serve as a model. We must be concerned for the whole girl and not just for her convenience.

Yet there is a further orthodox objection to the stance of the

New Morality and that is that it suffers from arrogance—the besetting characteristic of newness. It is arrogant because it demands of ordinary people the intellectual capacity of a John Robinson. It says to all of us—moral decisions must not only be prepared for by the quality of life. Each problem must be faced as a separate and unique issue to be wrestled with, without benefit of clergy or laws. It therefore places a premium upon intelligence which is totally at variance with the teaching of the carpenter's son from Nazareth. It also has the arrogance to assert that all the teachings of the great ethical figures in Christian history are wrong and that proponents of the New Morality are right. God evidently waited two thousand years to reveal that Christ had one Commandment too many and that thanks to twentieth century man and his permissive society we have found it out. This is the arrogance of all heretics of all time. They assume that theirs is a unique situation—all history is straining towards this point. They are able to put their finger on the one special interpretation of the Gospel which will bring people back to an understanding of the faith.

Yet surely the fact is that the Church has to face an age where the great need is to insist upon redressing the balance between stability and novelty and not to join the headlong rush after the new. The horror of the age is that all things are either new or of no use. Our mechanical method of diffusing news makes every passing change a phenomenon of universal importance available to the whole world through the voyeurism of television. The urgency of the signature tune of B.B.C. *News at Ten* or the C.B.S. News and the breathlessness of the B.B.C. *World at One* commentators imparts a spurious actuality and novelty even to reports of the latest in an innumerable list of heart transplants or another boring feat of endurance in a single-handed boat.

The Church must therefore be very careful that she is responding to the *needs* of modern man and not to his fashionable wants. He is obviously more likely to want the Christian package to be new. It would upset the whole pattern of importance of novelty and fashion if it were to be claimed that the ethical basis of life remains constant. If we were to be told that the moral laws could be applied to most situations and circumstances then there would be no profound novelty in

L

morality. This would not accord with today's psychological demands, particularly if we were to say that we do not stand much chance of applying moral laws satisfactorily unless we learn them and use them at all times in our lives. When the crunch comes, we are creatures of habit and unless we have practised morality in small things we are not likely to be able to face up to the great moral decisions.

This is indeed a hard saying for a civilization which lives by novelty but it does seem inescapable for the Christian. The Church is really not going to help the modern world if all that it does is to give a divine sanction to the system of morality which the world itself has evolved. There is a profound sense in which it is the Church's duty to lean away from the world in order to right the balance. In an age of Puritanism she ought to be seen to be charitable and in an age of licence she should hold fast to the Law. Unhappily she usually manages to learn the lesson so slowly that by the time she has got the emphasis right, society has changed radically and she has merely caught up with the new fashion. Once again Church and popular establishment are pulling in the same direction and the Church is reinforcing extremism and thereby underpinning error.

Of course the other reaction of the Church has been to take refuge in the old with no attempt at re-presentation nor any effort to see whether what we had always taken as essential was in fact merely an accretion. At least the New Morality men have taught us once again that we must see to it that we are not encumbering the faith with additions which we treat as essentials. Christian morality can never be reduced to law. Law uninformed by love has a Judaic harshness just as love uninformed by law is sentimentality. It is the complement of the static law and the ecstatic Love which is the unique offering of the Christian insight. Man, particularly religious man, finds all this rather difficult to take and is inclined to 'improve' it all by making interpretations, which are no part of the original, but which he soon assumes are of divine origin.

In no situation is this more clearly seen than in the difficulty Christian people have in distinguishing between what is proper for the State to require of its citizens and what the Church may ask of its faithful. The traditionalists do tend to believe that the State ought to take over from the Church a morality which it should then proceed to enforce or at very least which should be the basis of its social enactments. Such a confusion between what the State can properly demand and what the Church must ask, ignores the divine nature of the Church. The Church offers to the faithful the grace to live up to a standard which would be impossible without it. Its moral demands presuppose the regeneration of the people of God. It is, therefore, perfectly right when worldly people say that the State cannot demand of them Christian behaviour when they do not happen to be Christians. They say this because they do not want to be forced into a code which they do not accept. The Church should agree because it knows that the Christian code is unacceptable without the operation of grace. The law has little to do with Christian morality. At best it produces a grudging public uniformity, at worst the scandal of widespread disregard. There must be two standards. What the Church demands of its members and what a free society can demand of its people are different in kind as well as degree.

In the face of the permissive society the Church has got to decide on both its attitudes. It must continue to play its part in society in pressing for the proper legislation which will encourage the creation of a community which gives the citizen the best possible chance to make value judgements. It must continue to throw its weight behind the protection of the weak and it must take the lead in directing attention to the plight of those whom others have passed by. All that is its public duty. At the same time it has the vital job of seeing to it that the salt does not lose its savour but indeed is able to season the whole of life. This must mean that it continues to call upon Christians to accept a much higher calling than can be demanded of those who have not the faith. It can reasonably demand chastity where the State has no such right. It can uphold the indissolubility of marriage when society must make provision for divorce. It can outlaw homosexual practices as sinful, when the State can legalize them. The Church ought to demand a higher standard of its faithful and expect a different standard from the secular State.

It must, however, also be clear what standards it would expect the State to uphold and where it must fight to keep society open to the best. It must continue steadfast in promoting the sanctity of human life and that must mean that it should be intimately concerned in the arguments over abortion, euthanasia, and suicide. Although it must accept that the secular State cannot demand the indissolubility of marriage, it must care enough for the family to be totally involved in seeing that legislation on marriage and divorce does everything possible to protect the security of the marriage bond.

We shall look at these issues in detail as we come to them but there is a general matter which arises from them. The Church's reaction to the permissive society is not just determined by its assault on certain traditional Christian laws. The real point of conflict is much deeper than that. Permissiveness is one facet of a movement which suggests that the virtues of variety and excitement are to be preferred to those of continuity, stability, and discipline. In the parallel case of Victorian society the Church was presented with an attitude which precisely reversed the order. The result in the nineteenth century was hypocrisy and the result today is irresponsibility and triviality. In the nineteenth century the Church largely baptized the uncharitable morality of its day. It produced its version of 'the only ethic for "man come of age"' and thereby failed to make the specifically Christian witness which would have been to inform continuity, stability, and discipline with love. If today it follows Bishop Robinson it will fall into the reverse error and fail to inform love with continuity, stability, and discipline.

It is the nature of the leaven in the lump to supply life to the whole without which it would lose its creative possibilities. Victorian society could so easily stultify creativity, our own will whisk it away by indiscipline and submerge it in triviality. The Church has a basic duty here to insist on unchanging values. It cannot do that if it runs after an accommodation with the New Morality. In a very real sense it has a duty to oppose the fashionable quite deliberately so that men are not rushed away unthinkingly but are continually recalled to the claims of continuing standards.

This is the more important when the assault is upon stability for the Church must have a vested interest in a view of life which emphasizes the organic nature of society. The Christian faith is a faith for man living with his fellows. Its morality is

the morality of community. It cannot see an action as an
isolated case or as a private matter.

This is why we ought to question the findings of those whose
ethical views are situational. A good deal of discussion in this
area has centred around Harry Williams' contribution to that
seminal symposium from Cambridge, *Soundings*. He takes as his
examples two men who are characters in films. The first is a
sailor in *Never on Sunday* who is unsure of his ability to have
sexual intercourse and is helped to overcome his inhibitions
by a kindly prostitute. The other is the main character in
The Mark who has a history of being strongly attracted to
small girls because he is afraid of a fully-fledged emotional
involvement with a woman. Finally by the love and understanding of a woman he plucks up enough courage and they sleep
together and he finds that everything is all right.

Now any example is faulty but it is important to analyse these
two carefully because it is always with similar single examples
that those who maintain the importance of moral standards are
assailed. Harry Williams is saying two things about these situations. The first is that in both cases the women have been
charitable and have cleansed the men of something which
stopped them being whole personalities. The second is that
each of the men could well 'have disguised his fear by the cloak
of apparent morality. Like the Pharisees in the gospels and
many good churchmen today they might have been the victims
of unconscious hypocrisy, keeping the law as an insulation
against the living God, the Creator.'

The first point has been very well considered by Dr Trueman
Dicken in his book, *Loving on Principle*. He points out that there
is nothing in either example to prove the assertion that the
men were the better for their experience. The first and obvious
fact is that in either case the therapy might well not have
worked. As both are fictional the author could make sure that
everyone lived happily ever after but what would have been
the case if the sailor had found that he couldn't sleep with the
prostitute? Would that have put him off having a deep relationship with a woman for ever? It might have been that his background and upbringing would have made him emotionally
unable to do with a prostitute that which he was perfectly
well able to do with someone he loved. Might not her 'charity'

have then resulted in confirming him in his belief when in fact it was totally erroneous?

Similarly, the man who feared he was a pervert. What a disaster if he had not made it. How much more likely he would then have been to give up his struggle and run after little girls. How much less likely too that a single sexual encounter like this could succeed compared with the permanent liaison with a woman who was prepared to take this man in sickness and in health. In either case the charity of the women involved does seem fairly limited. They merely made themselves available for trial by ordeal. But even granted that both had summed up their men correctly and that the consummation was successfully achieved, what is the guarantee that this was morally advantageous? As Trueman Dicken suggests, it might have been a very good thing that the sailor was worried about his physical capability. Once he had removed that worry he might have rushed off begetting bastards all over Greece and the Mediterranean. Of course he might not, but it is a curious moral stand to take that, if one breaks the traditional moral code with the best of intentions, then all things will automatically work together for good. As for the man tempted by little girls, his future activities might likewise be much less Christ-like than is assumed. In any case the psychological sequence is fairly un-unconvincing and the inevitability of his complete recovery seems rather unlikely.

As for the two men themselves, here Harry Williams seems even less logical. He says they might have lived their lives as the victims of unconscious hypocrisy—thinking they kept the Law because they were righteous when in reality they were frightened to break it. Now this may well be so but surely it is an argument for their being honest with themselves and not one for their breaking the moral code. It is not fornication which revealed to them that they were frightened of normal sexual intercourse —it was because they knew that they were frightened that they fornicated. They could, therefore, hardly be the victims of *unconscious* hypocrisy if they had kept to the dictates of the moral code. The act of sexual intercourse had no bearing on their hypocrisy, unconscious or otherwise. It is surely not suggested that we have first to sin and enjoy it in order that our subsequent abstention from sin may be accounted virtuous. In any

case the only way that these two could be the 'victims of unconscious hypocrisy' would be if they were to glory in their
righteousness in keeping the Law and that is precisely what we
are taught not to do. The sin of the Pharisee was not that he
did the right thing for the wrong reasons but that he patted
himself on the back for doing some of the right things and forgot
about humility and charity. Christ was not condemning fasting
and keeping the Law, he was condemning those who gloried
in their ostentatious righteousness and failed actually to be good.
Neither of Harry Williams' men needed to have fornicated in
order to stop being hypocrites and both of them would have
been much more likely to have found the answer to their
particular problems had they opened themselves to the love of
God and sought a permanent relationship within which their
sexual potential could best be used.

On the other hand, if a permanent relationship did not come
about, it is just possible that God's plan for either of these
individuals did not include their marrying. It is again a curious
morality which accepts as axiomatic that sexual relations are so
important that if marriage is impossible then fornication is
better than nothing. That may well be the view of the permissive
society or of the misreaders of Freud. It cannot reasonably be
the view of the Christian.

Of course we have to be very careful in arguing cases, but
unfortunately the believers in situational morality very rarely
give us any option because they tend to say with Harry
Williams: 'Sexual intercourse outside marriage may be often,
perhaps almost always, an exploitation, unilateral, or mutual.
But there are CASES where it need not be and isn't.' Or with
Fletcher, 'an ethic is inauthentic until it gets down to cases'.
Therefore we have to take the cases which the situationists give
us and argue each one. What then seems usually to be true is
that the Christian must answer the situationist straight by
proving that the particular example does not stand up.
Christianity is a personal religion and love demands that people
are treated as individuals but never as individuals *in absentia*.
The Church must certainly be prepared to examine cases but
it does so in full awareness that it is concerned with man as an
individual within the community of God's creation. He is not
an island, he is his brother's keeper, and it may well be that

he has to suffer that others may be saved—after all, such is the Christian pattern.

This is a hard saying and it is particularly difficult for this age to accept. As Fletcher rightly says, 'Our milieu and era are far unfriendlier to law ethics than were the apostolic and patristic times to say nothing of the mediaeval period.' Yet the reason that it is unfriendly is because it is determined to remove God from the equation. It accepts that love is the greatest good and it rightly rejoices in the experiences of human love which we enjoy. God does not naturally come into the thinking but if he did, then it would be by reversing the great Christian claim so that it reads 'Love is God'. This is perfectly acceptable as long as you do not then go and interpret 'love' in so relative and shallow a way that it results in your limiting God to what human beings can know of him through their experience and your obedience to him in those situations in which you can see that he is right.

Yet, if the assault of the permissive society upon the Church has led some to see a New Morality more in tune with the times, its other major effect has been to produce a radical re-examination of the Christian attitude to society. Much of the irritation with the demands of the traditional moral code has arisen because such demands seem irrelevant and insignificant in a world faced with starvation, nuclear annihilation and rampant racialism. It is the fact that the world, and particularly the youth of the world, is vitally concerned with these issues and sublimely unconcerned with the issues which the Church has traditionally thought important, that has led many Christians to strident demands that the Church should be seen to be on the side of light in the great battles of our time.

Now this argument is superficially most attractive. We have seen how young people have seized upon the exterior morality involved, while casting aside the personal morality once demanded. Perhaps the Church could find a point of contact here and demonstrate its relevance to a sceptical world. If Christians were seen to be in the forefront of the popular move-ments against apartheid and for women's liberation then they might be taken seriously in other matters. This is a sort of variant on the soup-kitchen argument. Get them inside the kitchen because they find soup attractive, make them pleased with you because you are on their side, then they will start coming to sing hymns on Sunday. Like Percy Dearmer, who tried to re-introduce English country arts and crafts so that people would come folk-dancing back to Church, the Church supposes that by jumping on whatever bandwaggon happens to be going it will gather to itself supporters who can be turned into Christians.

In fact, of course, it usually makes itself look ridiculous. Experience of medieval theocracies and of the Pope's attempts to gain secular power should have taught the Church that it is not a political organization and that when it attempts to be such it is either laughable or positively dangerous. Nor does it matter that, in general, the Church's political initiatives are now on the side of revolution rather than the Establishment. In either case the Church's job is not to provide specific political answers to problems but to witness to the eternal truths of the Gospel—demanding of its faithful that they be guided by those truths in making their political judgements. The Archbishop of Canterbury is clearly right as a Christian leader to condemn racialism as contrary to the teaching of Christ. He has no business to draw from that a conclusion that to sell arms to South Africa is morally wrong. It must be a political judgement as to whether a particular act will or will not best serve the cause of freedom. The Church is right to emphasize the duty of Christians to do everything possible to stop the slaughter on the roads but that does not give it a right to pontificate on speed limits.

What Galileo said in his letter to the Grand Duchess Christina in 1613 applies to political judgement today as much as it did to scientific judgement then. 'Let us grant then that theology is conversant with the loftiest divine contemplation, and occupies the regal throne among the sciences by this dignity. But acquiring the highest authority in this way, if she does not descend to the lower and humbler speculation of the subordinate sciences and has no regard for them therefore they are not concerned with blessedness then her professors should not arrogate to themselves the authority to decide on controversies in professions which they have neither studied nor practised. Why, this would be as if an absolute despot, being neither a physician nor an architect, but knowing himself free to command, should undertake to administer medicines and erect buildings according to his whim—at grave peril of his poor patients' lives and the speedy collapse of his edifices.' The Church must distinguish between its continued duty to challenge men with the overriding demands of the Gospel and its constant temptation to tell men how to use their political judgement.

Yet it is precisely this kind of political judgement that many would wish the Church to make. We have recently had the spectacle of the British Council of Churches solemnly voting against the introduction of commercial radio as if they were a proper body to make such a judgement. By all means let them point to the concern they may have in the right ordering of communications media. Let them give evidence to any enquiry and let individual Christians take an active part in the discussions but this is not a matter of faith or morals and neither the Church nor the Churches has any business to pretend it is.

What is true of this relatively trivial example is just as true of the great issues. There is a Christian view on war. Apart from some total pacifists, it clearly allows that there are occasions upon which war is justified. It is the Church's duty to hold before our political leaders the moral challenges involved in any war and to press them to make their decisions in the context of the Gospel. It is not the business of the Church to judge whether a war is a 'holy' one or not. Just as we must think it wrong for the hierarchy to throw the weight of the Church behind a particular side so it really is unacceptable that the Church should condemn the war in Vietnam or seek to promote a particular series of peace moves.

All this would seem a perfectly obvious lesson from the history of the Church. What is curious, therefore, is that the breathless Left are quite happy to condemn the Church's political interference in Spain or in Italy today or its historic involvement in the statecraft of Europe, while being at the same time perfectly prepared to demand that it should make political pronouncements on Britain's policy on Rhodesia and the American involvement in Vietnam. Could it be that they are less concerned with the fact of the Church's interference and more interested in their belief that the Church had not interfered on the right side! From these same sources we have had a good deal of adverse comment on the fact that the Church has in the past backed the Christian Democrats in Italy but nothing but praise for the World Council of Churches' decision to send money to the terrorists and/or freedom fighters in Africa. The trouble is that neither position is a tenable one. The Church has no business to get involved in political judgements. It must not be forced to decide whether things have gone so far in South Africa that the only solution is bloodshed, nor to choose between the political parties in Italy. Its job is to continue to witness to the truth and point men to the context within which they ought to make their political judgements. It is a curious thing that at a time in which the Church is questioning its infallibility in matters of faith and morals it should be acting as if it had a special kind of infallible judgement in matters of politics.

Of course all this has arisen because the Church has been fundamentally challenged by the society in which it has had to operate. In previous years it may have been ignored or attacked but it was always sure of its own claim upon people. Today it has 'lost its nerve' and in refusing to continue its former rôle in society it is desperately looking for a new one. In one direction this has resulted in the quest for a new and more relevant morality and in the other in the demand that the Church should become a leader in the revolutionary battle. This last position has meant that the old myth of Christ the revolutionary leader has reared its head. There is practically no support for this view either in the Gospels or in the tradition of the Church but it would be very convenient for those who see that the Church should prove its relevance by espousing every advanced cause. One group of clergy in the Southwark diocese in England, agreed that there was no sign of this side of Christ in the Bible and took refuge in the answer that of course the Gospels were an incomplete account of his life and that therefore it was acceptable to infer it.

In fact, Christ was the opposite of a revolutionary leader and took great pains to show men that his Kingdom was not of this world but was revolutionary in the most fundamental of all senses in that it sought to bring about a change in the hearts of people. It asked that they should be born again not that they should overthrow Caesar. Indeed it was specifically this tempta-tion in the wilderness to which he refused to succumb. He did not accept that his mission was to win the kingdoms of the world. His was to change the hearts of men and to do that he would not fall down and worship the devil. Sadly all this is not immediate enough for many of the leaders of the Church. They are not prepared to accept their rôle as those who change men through the Word and the Sacraments. That seems not relevant enough so they must join in with the competing political clamour on every side and by so doing worship the devil in his belief that the kingdom of God can be brought about by political action. Their spiritual forbears are the Crusaders and the Inquisition and their danger is that they will tie the Church to political judgements which will seem in fifty years' time as erroneous as those of Richard Coeur de Lion or the Duke of Alva.

Not that this must mean that the Church is not involved in the world. It has an essential rôle in building both the Christian and the secular society. Its claims upon the faithful are claims which can only be made in the context of the grace which it offers in the Word and the Sacraments. They are different and much more onerous demands than those which can be made by any human authority. At the same time it has the duty to recall the secular society continually to the standards and values which it upholds. President Nixon must not be allowed to become complacent about the war in Vietnam, nor Prime Minister Heath about racialism in South Africa. The Church must be the leaven in the lump, continually informing the consciences of the politicians. Faith and morals are the sphere of the Church, the secular leader must make political judgements for himself.

Nor is it true that the Church has some sort of vested interest in anarchy or revolution. Palestine was in a revolutionary situation when Christ brought the Gospel message. Yet he still called upon people to render unto Caesar that which was Caesar's. It was indeed within the order of the Roman Empire that the Church made its great headway. The Church has always seen in order the opportunity man needs to be fully himself. When secular order breaks down, then the Church has to create its own order so that its life may continue. This was the greatness of St Benedict who saw that as the Roman Empire fell apart, he had to create a community which was able to withstand the pressures from without. It is therefore no wonder that the Benedictines had vows of poverty, chastity, and *stability*.

What we see about us now is a determined attempt to put the values of disorder first. This is to attack the ideal worldly situation in which there is tension between the opposite values. In a society where the importance of order and the vitalizing effect of change and variety is kept in balance, then creativity can have its way. The Church is essentially a creative body. It is reconciling man to God, showing him forth on earth, and being eternally the leaven in the lump. Its concept of society must therefore be one where personal responsibility is encouraged. The society of violence and continuous revolution can hardly be conducive to responsibility or to the creation of community. The Church must therefore find itself always against those elements which would break up the community. It must be concerned that the State should recognize its duty to foster the family and to protect the community from the excesses of individuals, in the moral as well as the economic sphere.

It is the responsibility of the Christian lay leader to see how best this can be put into practice but he must be able to rely upon the Church continually to uphold the ideal upon which his actions must be based. To do this the Church must regain its nerve. Its job of witnessing to the truth and changing the hearts of men is surely the most immense task of all. It requires that the faith should be presented in a meaningful way and that the lives of believers should be such that they will demand imitation. It will mean that many individual Christians will see it as their duty to take the lead in many of the great social movements but it cannot mean that the Church should betray either its faith or its mission by seeking to change its teaching to fit the mood of the moment or espouse progressive or reactionary causes which seem likely to bring it favour and fortune. It must, instead, uphold the principle of individual judgement informed by the teaching of the corporate body in matters of faith and morals.

And there is no doubt that the individual needs every bit of help he can get. The effect of the change in our society has been to call into question every standard of judgment which previously seemed unassailable. Chief among these has been the overwhelming importance of the sanctity of human life. Against this fundamental principle, campaigns in the Western world for abortion, euthanasia, and legal suicide were all unsuccessful until this present decade. Today the secular State is just beginning to take stock of the new position and is finding it very difficult indeed.

10 Towards a new Community

We have seen how the drug addict outrages society, by denying the secular world's one essential dogma—the overwhelming importance of self-preservation. In an age which has freed itself from sexual taboos only to take on a whole lot more about death, people who knowingly kill themselves are hitting society where it hurts most. They shout loud and clear—'we don't want your world and we'll show you by dropping out, not just by refusing to accept the inconveniences, like the work-shy or the delinquent, but right out by refusing to worship at the secular shrine of self-preservation.' This has alway been the ultimate assertion of dissent—to accept death, rather than life on society's terms.

Now of course it is often not as simple or as high-flown as that, yet invariably, somewhere in the drug addict's cry for help is the belief that society has included him out, and that there is no place for him within the community. Indeed, for many of the intelligent, the situation is more universal than that. For them society is organized in such a way as to exclude, by its very nature, the addict and others who feel that they do not belong. As the straight world does not seem to include him, he finds his community among those rejected because of their common dependence. In denying the normal society he clings to the group identification which drug-taking provides.

It is therefore not surprising that the only successful way to wean people from drugs is to provide a community which replaces the shared experience of addiction—the badge of belonging—by the realization of a new belonging to a community, bound together by the common problem of staying off drugs. The addict's cry for help can only be answered within a society whose common life can sustain him where he is weak and increasingly bring out his talents, reassuring him of his worth to his fellows.

The sad thing is that we need a special community for surely it is precisely what society ought to do for all of us.

The whole concept of community must be that it takes the strain from the individual where he is unable to bear it and provides sufficient assurance of his worth to see that he uses his talents to the common good. Man is in a very deep sense a social animal. He was never meant to stand on his own feet. He was meant to capitalize on his good points, contribute to the community as he was able, and rely upon others whose talents lay in different fields to help him where he was weak. It is the universal principle of barter which lies at the heart of family and community life. Within the extended family or village community, the individual is not isolated or submerged. He has his assured place within a framework of inter-dependence. As he relies on others, they rely on him. He belongs. The gossip may be wearisome, the lack of privacy inhibiting, and the danger of claustrophobia continual; but he belongs.

If he fails in childhood and adolescence to get on with his parents, he can turn to others for satisfactory relationships. The extended family and the neighbours eliminate the worst of the generation gap. The security of community can take the strain of the tension between young and old, the new and the traditional. The rebel and the wanderer will disappear, he will need the challenge of new places and new things, but for most, the frenzied presentation of the new, the insistence upon variety and change cannot be coped with except against a stable and continuing background of community. It is the common experience of the permissive society that its citizens do not belong. The challenge of the permissive society is the challenge of community. As one of the young people building a commune in the U.S.A. said to William Hedgepath: 'this world is doomed—the next stage is community'.

If then the creation of a real community is the answer, the Western world will need to do an about-turn pretty smartly. The whole tendency of modern capitalism is towards the destruction of such community as does exist. We have seen the effects of the frenetic exploitation of the new which is so essential a part of the marketing strategy of mass production. New public housing and the tearing down of the slums paradoxically destroys rather than promotes community.

The sheer size of our cities creates loneliness and the pressure put upon our citizens to compete for material possessions has already destroyed the concept of the extended family and is now busy pulling the nuclear family of parents and young children apart as women rush out to work to earn enough to keep up with the Joneses.

And it is with the family that we must start. The results of investigation into the mental and physical growth of children are very inconvenient for the progressive school. It must be a great blow to the Women's Liberation Front to discover how important it is for the mother of a family to be at home, creating a stable environment in which her children can grow to maturity. The advocates of easy divorce and sequential polygamy must find the news of the frightening effects of family instability during the early life of a child and even during pregnancy, most shattering. Even the moderate supporters of the notion that women must be able to carry on a life independent of the home while the children are growing up, can hardly be entirely happy with the evident effects that this has had upon so many 'latch-key' children.

Of course it would be wrong to suggest that because of this women should by nature be predestined to remain at home to cope with the children and denied the right to make a career for themselves. It is clearly not true that all women are happiest in the home and many are likely to create instability within the family if forced to remain full-time housewives.

What we have to ask, however, is whether it is sensible for society to be so structured that it makes it positively difficult for women to remain at home, bringing up a family. The consumer revolution, with its convenience foods, washing machines and miracle cleaners, has provided the means whereby women can go out to work and the pressure is often on them to do so. The affluent society exists because so many families have two pay packets. Women leave the dreary round of household chores in order to go out and be paid for the often dreary round of repetitive work. The one advantage, apart from the money, is the company of others similarly engaged. Yet to hear the feminists talk, you would think that married women consisted exclusively of doctors and writers for glossy magazines, penned in doing the washing-up. In fact, in the majority of cases, going out to work is really a matter of wanting the company and the money. If this is so, then it is a pity that society has increasingly arranged

M

itself so that neither is available to the woman in the home. The decline of the family to a narrowly self-contained unit of parents and young children, has meant that women have lost the society of the extended family; at the same time there is much more rarely someone else in the home who can take on the rôle of bringing up the family for women who really do find that rôle inimical. The grandmother or aunt living near by so frequently provided that stability which enabled the wife to pursue a life outside the home.

Dr Spock is perfectly right when he highlights the problem of the working mother and insists that society ought to find a way of paying the mother to stay at home. Instead we have a society in which the average family's material expectations can only be satisfied if both parents go out to work. We are paying dearly for this in social terms.

However, it is possible to change the situation. In our housing policies we should preserve the extended families which still remain. In rehousing schemes there is no reason why long-established communities should not be recreated in better conditions rather than split up as individuals and families and sent to different areas. Our insistence upon treating the nuclear family as the basis for rehousing must be overcome. Public housing authorities ought increasingly to provide accommodation suitable for those with aged parents or other relatives. How much better for old people to have a self-contained one-roomed flat close by the maisonette provided for their children, rather than being tidied away in a block of 'senior citizens' accommodation' presided over by a warden.

We could also use the taxation system to lessen the incentive for two-income families by increasing the allowances made in respect of the non-working mother. Above all, we could begin to plan for communities rather than building individual housing units, so that the woman in the home would feel part of a society instead of being isolated and immured.

This kind of planning is, of course, all part of a much bigger problem. We have tended to think that given decent conditions in which to live, people will create their own community. In fact, it is in the huge new housing complexes that people are most isolated and the young most at a loss. In Europe and America, public housing has tended to perpetuate and solidify class differences. Council housing estates have become one-class societies from which the successful children move away and into which young low-income families are continually moving. No doctors or teachers, architects or executives, live in this community. The local schools often serve the area exclusively and therefore promote little mixing of different classes.

Just as destructive are the smart suburbs with their neat semi-detached houses or miniature colonial-style homes. No public housing here, only the owner-occupier. Plenty of doctors, teachers, architects, and businessmen, but no plumbers, wood-workers, or joiners. Increasingly, both areas are left to parents and young children as the teenagers leave home to live separate lives among other young people. The old are put away in homes and little flats. In America, whole townships reserved for the over-fifty-fives are springing up and others are appearing aimed at single people, or young married couples, or couples with children. This is merely to formalize what has happened in many parts by accident.

Much of Florida, like the south coast of England, has for a long time been 'reserved' for the retired. Society cannot stop people choosing to live with others of their own age or of similar background and interests. What it can do is to prevent such divisions being inevitable. Public housing ought to be carried on in partnership with private development so that instead of creating vast estates of low-cost housing, we build mixed developments catering for a much wider range of families. Public authorities could certainly insist that a proportion of the homes in private developments be made available for their housing needs. The policy to sell existing council housing which has been pioneered by Conservative-controlled councils in Great Britain points the way to undoing some of the harm already done in the creation of 'unmixed' estates. New developments of public building should provide accommodation suitable for extended families, as well as homes for people such as teachers and doctors who will serve the community. Gradually we could begin to make the kind of mixed society which a real community needs, although it will be a long and extremely difficult programme. Authorities like Tower Hamlets in London and New York City, who are acutely aware of the sheer physical problem of rehousing from slum conditions will find it difficult to adjust to the proposition that some of their resources must go into building a real community. Tower Hamlets has seen to it that there has been practically no private development in that area of London since the war. Instead their ideal has been totally council-owned housing stock. They refuse to sell homes to their tenants and education in the area is considerably hampered because teachers can find nowhere to live. The motive of decent housing for all is good, but the effect is terrifying. In an area of ghetto-like estates, the schools are socially no more comprehensive than a girls' finishing school. What can teachers who come in from outside the area do to change or improve the one all-pervasive life-style?

So we must face the problems of our inner cities. In America and in Europe, urban renewal can only be made a reality if we ensure that our city centres once again become live communities with proper provisions for all kinds of people. It cannot be right to perpetuate a situation in which either these parts are left to run down so that only the deprived can tolerate the conditions or they become areas where only the very rich can afford to live. In Britain, cost-yardsticks for local authority building must be varied to allow for building homes as well as shops in central developments. America ignores the lessons of Europe at her peril. As she comes to grips with the problems of her decaying city centres she will achieve nothing if she only reproduces the same one-class community living in rather better packages. Our cities can only live if we are prepared to break them down into neighbourhoods small enough to have meaning for those who live there, but comprehensive enough to include people of all types.

Yet if we have to build and plan for community, we also have to educate for it. It is through education that society hands on to the next generation that which it feels is valuable and ought to be preserved. It is of necessity, therefore, a paternal process. Society chooses what is to be taught and the educational system reflects the values which it sees as important. Sometimes those values are not noticeably upheld outside the school environment; only 10 per cent of people in Britain go to church but well over 80 per cent of parents want religious knowledge taught in schools! This double standard does not make the teacher's job any easier but a society will often recognize what it wants for the next generation, while denying it for itself. All Western societies see education as fulfilling this major function of training the young in what has been found to be valuable. In Britain, when venereal disease and illegitimacy have reached epidemic proportions, the immediate demand is—'what are the schools doing about it'. In the U.S.A. with its frightening growth in drug abuse, it is the schools which are seen as the first line in society's fight against the problem.

What is true of the moral is as true in the academic. The educational system has traditionally been the way in which the young assimilated the whole pattern of knowledge which has shaped the society in which they have been born. The primacy of the classics and, latterly, the importance of history, are witness to this desire that the young should understand what it is that has shaped society. At the same time, their minds have been brought into contact with great minds of the past, not only to challenge their assumptions, but also to temper their natural arrogance by pointing out that others have reached the pinnacles without the advantage of currently fashionable doctrines.

Yet today these basic assumptions are being challenged by some educationists. They see the school, not as a place where the young learn the world's wisdom, but rather as somewhere where they express themselves. The concept of a community upholding certain values and instilling certain truths has been replaced by one in which the individual is given every opportunity to express his own views. The aim is to create a generation of assertive and critical people who are not afraid to challenge the commonly held views of their society. It is a noble aim and one which would certainly have been part of the best of traditional education. Unfortunately, it is increasingly the *only* aim of education and as such is thoroughly dangerous.

We must beware of creating a generation which is able to criticize and challenge, not from knowledge, but only from ignorance. Our elevation of the principle of spontaneity into a universal good, and our fear of 'learning by rote' have begun to create an attitude which dismisses altogether the importance of learning and knowledge. It is important to examine the reason for this change.

At the heart of the matter lies the revolution in teaching methods. Once the magister was a figure of authority who imparted knowledge to his pupils and they learned what he asked upon pain of punishment. The arrangement of the old schoolroom illustrates this graphically. The teacher's desk upon a dais and the boys facing him as he told them what was what; 'Chalk and talk', as it is now disparagingly called. The change in the physical arrangement of classrooms mirrors the change in attitudes. The pupils sit much less formally and the teacher moves among them, helping out where necessary. The silence which was considered vital in former days has been replaced by the 'creative noise' of children working on their projects, finding out more of the world in which they live.

This change in technique was, of course, a purely practical one. As the schools realized their obligation to educate everybody, and not merely the academically bright, it became clear that children learned very little formally unless they were determined and willing. For most pupils it was only by engaging their attention through project teaching and creative work that they would learn what was required.

Yet this change is more fundamental than it would seem at first sight. As long as it is a learning technique, then the project concept is most valuable. However, it has begun to affect the ends of education. We are in danger of selecting what is to be learned, not because it is intrinsically valuable, but because it fits more easily into the new methods.

Now the things least naturally suited to these techniques are precisely those things which have traditionally been most important in education. Project teaching is by its very nature discursive and superficial. It lends itself, not to the disciplined study of the classics or of academic history but to the simplistic deductions of social studies and popular social history. It certainly enables children to find out for themselves and is therefore a valuable tool, but it cannot replace the disciplined approach of academic study. Now the 'progressives' amuse themselves in attacking 'learning by rote' and thereby miss the point. It is not that the new methods are to be attacked *per se*. It is that they must not blind us to the need for the kind of education which stretches the child's mind by the discipline of real scholarship.

Nor must we allow modern teaching systems to engender an

attitude which despises real research and knowledge. There is a tendency for pupils' opinions to be given an importance which they do not have, simply because they have arrived at them through their own research. If that research has been faulty or superficial then it may well be that the views based upon it are wrong. Many teachers are reluctant to say so in case it discourages or, more dangerously, because they are not prepared to pass judgement. This whole attitude denies the vital function of the teacher as the person who hands on that which society holds valuable. The teacher is not there merely to excite his pupils' interest in the world around him, he is there to give them some canons of judgement against which they can measure what they learn and also to introduce them to the heritage of a civilization.

In doing this, the educator is preparing the young for community. He is giving them a common frame of references and allowing them to enter in upon a common experience. They may, of course, react against what they have learned, but at least they will be fully aware of what it is they are rejecting. Without this element in education the young are denied everything except that which is easily available. They are denied the discipline and the real pleasure of wrestling with the problems which have vexed men for generations. It is not therefore surprising that they tend to imagine that the questions which they ask and answer with such aplomb are new. Instead of understanding how others have tackled the issues, they assume that all previous generations have been insensitive and unable to understand and they all too easily fall prey to those with a smattering of knowledge which they parade as proof. We do need to make sure that the next generation fully understands that which we have found to be valuable in our heritage. It is necessary if the community is to survive because it provides the link between generations. It provides a common framework within which people of different ages can rationally talk. Above all, it sees that each new generation does not have to start again at the beginning but can share together the common experience of the civilization into which they have been born.

We have, therefore, to insist that both project teaching and academic instruction should form part of our educational scene. This in turn means that the teacher must continue to uphold to a degree his traditional rôle as mentor. He cannot contract out, suggesting that he is in no position to set standards and demand obedience. Many teachers in American schools have refused to take a lead on the drugs question because they consider it something which children must be left to decide for themselves. One drug addiction specialist visiting a fashionable private school was told by the teachers that they found it difficult to censure the children for using cannabis because they used it themselves and it would be hypocritical to deny them what they allowed themselves. The staff was very taken aback to be told that they had no business to be using cannabis and that it was part of the responsibility of anyone who set themselves up as a teacher to regulate their private lives so that they could with honesty demand of pupils the highest of standards. This was considered unacceptable interference in the private life of an individual. Yet surely it is perfectly reasonable for society to ask of those which it entrusts with the education of the next generation, that they themselves accept the discipline imposed by the standards which they ought to impart.

The pressure among pupils for more democracy in schools is to be welcomed in so far as it is attacking the arbitrary refusals and unnecessary restrictions which have traditionally been the way of schoolmasters. Yet any assertions that it is the duty or the ability of those under instruction to decide in what they are to be instructed or how syllabuses are to be managed is to deny the right and purpose of the community which is to educate according to its values and standards. The new generation may dislike them and deny them but it will do so the more effectively if it first understands them.

Thus the community has a duty to see that no one is denied the right of sharing in the heritage of society. The modern methodology of education must not be allowed to usurp the ends of education, nor must the schoolmaster refuse to accept his place as mentor. Society must not lose its nerve. It cannot avoid its duty to educate the next generation no matter how great the pressures, particularly in the universities, may be. The recent campus troubles which have swept the world present us with a major problem. They are the extreme manifestation of a growing intolerance among certain sections of young people to any views save their own. Like most large movements, the causes are by no means simple. There is no doubt that university administration in many countries has signally failed to meet the needs of this generation. In France, for example, the university population has more than doubled, while there has been practically no extension of facilities.

Similarly in Germany the style and attitude of university authorities had hardly changed since before the war. In America it took some time for university authorities to face up to the change in their students from the rather conformist attitudes which so surprised Europeans in the fifties. There has been very urgent need for reform in many Western countries and many complaints of students have been justified.

Nor must we forget the traditional and proper rôle of the student radical. The battles of medieval times between town and gown and between masters and students had much in common with today's unrest and if we believe in the creative tension between the established order and the challenge posed by a new generation, then we must welcome much of this dissent.

Yet to welcome dissent and to concede to it are two different things and there is a disturbing tendency among university authorities to abdicate their position in the face of minority protest. Society does need to see that its own educational purposes are not swamped by the fashionable demands of groups of students. It also has the duty to hold the ring so that fascists —black or red—cannot restrict the freedom of students to hear any views they like. It is a sad fact in British universities that the total freedom of speech which was available ten years ago has now been very severely curtailed because of the activities of the student militants.

I remember debating with Sir Oswald Mosley, the British Fascist leader, in front of an audience of 2,000 in Cambridge. They gave all the speakers a fair hearing but the Jewish leaders had, of course, made sure that I had all the evidence I needed to see that people were fully aware of Mosley's activities. Today there is no chance that such a meeting would be held. Early in 1971 the Cambridge University Conservative Association had invited the British Home Secretary to speak. Reginald Maudling is a man of moderate and liberal views but because he had felt it right not to renew the visa of the German student radical, Rudi Dutschke, there was a good deal of feeling against him.

The hotel where Sir Oswald Mosley had been entertained ten years previously was the usual meeting-place of the University Conservative Association and yet the management felt that the danger of violence was so great that it could not allow the Home Secretary to speak. What was far worse was that the University made no real effort to find an alternative venue and indeed prominent among those who opposed the Maudling visit were senior members of the university staff. Finally it was left to a local independent school to come to the rescue because the headmaster thought this was a matter of major principle.

Now this incident is small in itself but it illustrates the situation clearly. Here a small minority of students were out, not to argue with an opponent, but to prevent him speaking. Instead of the university authorities insisting that facilities be given so that the refusal of a private company to provide a room should not jeopardize the proper expression of views, they would not take a stand.

This refusal only perpetuates the sad situation in which strong-arm tactics can deny freedom of even moderate speech in a university which a short time ago would have welcomed anyone, however extreme his views. What is true here in principle is paralleled by the situations in riot-torn campuses in the U.S.A., in other British universities where bricks have been thrown at unpopular guest speakers and paint poured over their companions, as well as in the more complex conditions of Continental universities.

In every case, society has a right to demand that freedom of speech is preserved not just because, generally speaking, it contributes to the cost of the university, but more important, because the university is society's instrument of educating a new generation and the conditions in which it is able to operate effectively are a proper subject of communal concern.

This concern should be not only to establish and maintain reasonable order within which the university can operate, but also to see that there are objective standards by which people are judged and according to which they are taught. There is a growing demand that syllabuses should be determined by the students and that external examinations at all points in the educational system should be abolished. There is much to be said for a continual and extensive overhaul of curricula and examination systems. There are many sides to education which cannot easily be examined and therefore tend to be ignored by the schools. There are clear anomalies in examinations and many university courses should be rethought.

Yet apart from all this, there is a major principle which must not be forgotten. An important task of the educational system is to pass on to the new generation that which it considers valuable in civilization. By its nature that can only be decided upon by those who have learned rather than those who are learning; it is unacceptable that a first year biology student should decide what it is suitable for him to learn. It is no less ludicrous in the case of the arts. Education is essentially undemocratic in practice and yet profoundly democratic in outcome. The concept of *status pupillari* is a very real one. Those with the knowledge impart it to those who would learn. The process may mean that both pupil and master gain new insights but there should really be no doubt as to who is directing the operation. At no time has it been more important to insist upon the truth of this. Jack is not as good as his master and it is the pretence that he is which is bedevilling much of our educational system, and through it, much of our society.

We have begun to despise the principle that there are objective standards. Teachers often insist that children should never feel they fail examinations, but merely that they pass at a lower level! This may have some validity when examinations are taken by a young child at a point when he may give an uncharacteristic account of himself and therefore be unnecessarily discouraged. It has no validity if it is used to suggest that academic excellence is no better than academic failure. By all means let us reform our examination systems in order to remove excessive rigidity, but it would be entirely wrong to remove from them the principle of the objective testing of academic knowledge. To do so might please those who value opinion above facts or who place self-expression above the importance of what is expressed by others, but it will not advance the cause of real education. It will not help us to create a community if we surrender the right to educate the next generation according to the values and standards which we find important. It will be for them to change and adapt those standards but they must first learn them.

Yet whatever future generations may do, the present fact is that the re-creation of our society lies in our own hands. We are steadily building a way of life which is intolerable for more and more people. It is one which does not commend itself to an important section of the new generation. Now that is partially because no way of life ever has, such is the nature of youth, but it is also because we have been less than effective in our attempts to present it to the young. Even more important, we seem not to have noticed that the effects of economic change over the past three decades have been to tear apart the whole basis upon which Western liberal democracy rested. Furthermore, the cult of youth and the destruction of the notion of authority have made it ever more difficult to maintain a framework of order.

Nor will it become any easier unless we see that society becomes community. We can no longer tolerate a civilization whose social organization removes power further and further from the people. We have got to effect a strengthening of the real units of society—those which are understood by all. The family, not in its modern selfish sense, but in the wider sense of the clan and the neighbourhood, no longer a one-class community, dominated by one age group, but more akin to the mixed community of the village.

In a society where people feel the strength and value of these institutions which touch them most closely, there can emerge an effective and real alternative to the principle of continual revolution. It is in this atmosphere that we can resume the real relationship between young and old from which the evolution of the community stems.

Such a community would be bound to demand from its members a much greater participation in the direction of their work. It would promote the welfare of individuals by seeing that they were increasingly capital-owning and thus had a stake in the economic fortunes of their society as well as some personal independence. This evolution will be a slow and painful process but it does provide an alternative to the twin juggernauts of modern capitalism and modern socialism.

Both systems create a society which, although materially improving, makes life increasingly intolerable for large numbers of its citizens. The mental breakdowns and the inadequate families, the increase in violence and the incidence of drug-taking—all demand that we initiate a radical change in the conditions of life in the Western world.

In that change the Church has an important part to play. It is in a real sense the archetypal community and it is a standing rebuke to modern Christians that the world would never say of them what was said in the first century A.D.—'see how those Christians love one another'. The emphasis throughout Christian writings has been to equate the Church and the family as the two societies ordained by God, and Christianity has always been an essentially corporate religion. Today, perhaps more than ever, it will be in the rediscovery of its nature as a community that the Church will be able to be the leaven in society's lump. That will not be possible if its whole attitude continues to be to seize upon the values of the world and make them its own. We desperately need a new St Benedict who, faced with the disintegration of the society he knew, drew together a Christian community which survived the onslaught of the barbarians and lived on to inform and civilize the new society which was to emerge.

The permissive society ought to be but a passing phase. It has struck against all the commonly held assumptions which having served liberal democracy for so long were felt to be part of the essential pattern of life. The assault is well worth while. It has made us face up to the fact that the sanctity of human life, the importance of the family, the very principle of order itself—all these are not universal principles, readily and completely accepted by all. They are principles that have to be thought out and re-applied in every new situation. It is simply not enough for society to assume their worth and expect their acceptance.

The challenge has been thrown down. We cannot return to the cosy and comfortable assumptions of pre-war days nor can we move into the arid society which denies all that we have thought valuable in the past. The only real way forward is for us to breathe new life into the principles we claim we hold. If they are to become real then they must be reflected in the sort of society which we create. We can no longer tolerate the isolation and non-participation of the contemporary world. That world is doomed. The next stage is community.